THE PERILOUS SEARCH FOR THE FABLED NORTHWEST PASSAGE IN AMERICAN HISTORY

The In American History Series

THE PERILOUS SEARCH FOR THE FABLED NORTHWEST PASSAGE IN AMERICAN HISTORY

Karen Clemens Warrick

Enslow Publishers, Inc.
40 Industrial Road   PO Box 38
Box 398   Aldershot
Berkeley Heights, NJ 07922   Hants GU12 6BP
USA   UK
http://www.enslow.com

Library of Congress Cataloging-in-Publication Data

Warrick, Karen Clemens.
    The perilous search for the fabled Northwest Passage in American
history / Karen Clemens Warrick.
        p. cm. — (In American history)
    Includes bibliographical references and index.
    Contents: Franklin's final voyage—Search for a new trade route—Brave
explorers in small ships—Sir John Barrow's push for arctic exploration—
Overland search for the Northwest Passage—Four winters in the Arctic—
Along the coast of North America—Search and discovery—Navigating the
passage—The Northwest Passage on the map.
    ISBN 0-7660-2148-3
    1. Northwest Passage—Discovery and exploration—Juvenile literature.
2. Arctic regions—Discovery and exploration—Juvenile literature.
3. Explorers—Northwest Passage—History—Juvenile literature.
4. Explorers—Arctic regions—History—Juvenile literature. [1. Northwest
Passage. 2. Arctic regions—Discovery and exploration. 3. North
America—Discovery and exploration. 4. Explorers.] I. Title. II. Series.
G640.W37   2004
910'.9163'27—dc22
                                        2003026603

Printed in the United States of America

10 9 8 7 6 5 4 3 2 1

To Our Readers: We have done our best to make sure all Internet Addresses in
this book were active and appropriate when we went to press. However, the
author and the publisher have no control over and assume no liability for the
material available on those Internet sites or on other Web sites they may link to.
Any comments or suggestions can be sent by e-mail to comments@enslow.com or
to the address on the back cover.

Illustration Credits: The Albert and Shirley Small Special Collections
Library, University of Virginia Library, p. 40; Canadian National Library,
pp. 15, 72, 88, 96, 113; © Corel Corporation, pp. 31 109; Enslow
Publishers, Inc., pp. 6, 102; From the collection of Russell A. Potter,
p. 17; George Back/National Archives of Canada, pp. 59, 60, 61; John
Webber/National Archives of Canada, p. 39; National Archives of
Canada, pp. 46, 50; Negelen/National Archives of Canada, p. 9;
Reproduced from the Collections of the Library of Congress, pp. 22, 35,
42; Samuel Gurney Cresswell/National Archives of Canada, p. 91.

Cover Illustration: Reproduced from the Collections of the Library
of Congress (large vertical photo); George Back/National Archives of
Canada/C-089481 (bottom horizontal photo); Negelen/National
Archives of Canada/C-001352 (small vertical photo); Samuel Gurney
Cresswell/National Archives of Canada/C-016105 (top horizontal
photo).

★ CONTENTS ★

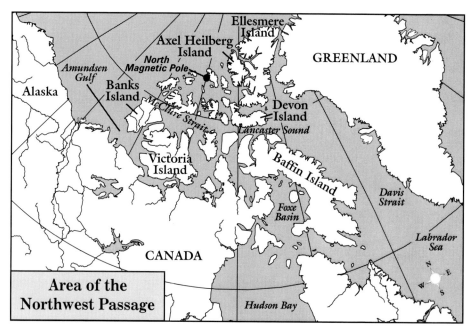

Over hundreds of years, many explorers would try to conquer the North American Arctic region in order to find passage to Asia through the Arctic Ocean.

FRANKLIN'S FINAL VOYAGE

On May 19, 1845, Jane Franklin watched as her husband sailed down the Thames River. Sir John Franklin was the captain of a British expedition. Its goal was to find the Northwest Passage. Lady Jane knew the voyage was important, but she still worried.[1]

John Franklin, now fifty-nine years old, had experience in the Arctic region. The explorer had surveyed Canada's northern coastline. He made two overland missions in 1819–1822 and 1825–1827. Preparations for his latest voyage began in February.

Franklin was given two large warships, *Erebus* and *Terror*. In addition to sails, both ships were equipped with steam engines. These twenty- and twenty-five-horsepower engines were the most modern way to power ships at that time. The energy they provided was not great, but could be an important resource to escape danger. When the wind died, sails were useless. The steam engines could then be fired up. Their power might move the ships through an opening in the pack ice and keep them from being crushed. Franklin also believed these new engines would be strong enough to force the ships through icy Arctic passages.[2]

The two ships were stocked with china, a library of books, dress uniforms, and mahogany furniture. Enough canned goods and supplies to last three years were crammed into the holds. Franklin had no plans to hunt for game in the icy wilderness. They also carried equipment for Arctic exploration.

The sailors were eager to sail under Franklin's command. One crew member wrote: "Sir John is delightful, active, and energetic. . . . He is full of . . . interesting anecdotes of his former voyages. I would not lose him for the command [have him replaced], for I have a real regard, I might say affection, for him, and believe this is felt by all of us."[3]

By July, the ships reached Cape Farewell on the southern tip of Greenland. A storm forced them to shelter near some islands. From there, Franklin wrote a letter to his wife. He told her not to worry if he did not return after the first winter. Then his expedition sailed north following the coast of Greenland.

Near the end of July, two whaling ships sighted the expedition. Franklin's ships were anchored beside an iceberg, collecting data. The whaler's captain reported that Franklin and his crew were well and in good spirits. They were headed toward Lancaster Sound, a waterway west of Greenland and north of Baffin Island. John Franklin expected to finish the voyage in excellent time.

Sir John Franklin set sail on May 19, 1845, in search of the Northwest Passage.

Then two winters passed with no more news from the expedition. Lady Jane waited. She told herself there was no reason to worry. Sir John had expected to spend a second winter in the Arctic region.

Most people gave little thought to the lack of news about Franklin's expedition. Other world events held their attention. Americans were at war with Mexico. The floor of the Atlantic Ocean was being surveyed. Engineers were working on plans to lay a telegraph cable from New York to Ireland.

Missing

By the summer of 1847, there was still no word from Franklin's expedition. Lady Jane asked the Royal Navy to search for her husband. Sir John Ross, another experienced Arctic explorer, was also concerned. He pointed out that Franklin's supplies would be running low by now. However, expeditions often stayed more than two years in the Arctic region. Officials were not alarmed. They refused to send ships to search. They did order Hudson's Bay Company to take special stocks of food to northern trading posts. These supplies would be waiting for Franklin's expedition, if they had to trek overland across the Canadian Arctic region.

By spring of 1848, all of Great Britain began to worry. An entire expedition was missing—two ships and 134 men. The government offered a reward of twenty thousand British pounds for Franklin's rescue. Anyone with news of the expedition would be paid half that amount. Inuit in northern Canada were asked to watch for the ships. Lady Franklin also offered a reward. She promised two thousand pounds (then about ten thousand dollars) for any information about her husband.

Though it might be too late, the British Royal Navy decided to send ships out to search. This was easier said than done. Where would they begin searching? The navy examined Franklin's original plans to see where he had expected to go. It was necessary to guess which direction he had sailed. Weather and ice conditions would have determined the actual course. The territory they needed to search was enormous, and for the most part, unexplored.

The Search

Three years after Franklin had sailed, the first expedition left England in June 1848. It was under the command of Sir James Ross, an old friend of Franklin. Francis Leopold McClintock was one of the crew members. He was young and eager to study the Arctic region. During the journey, McClintock learned to travel overland using Inuit dog sleds. He also learned to communicate using Inuktitut, the Inuit language.

Ross and his ships attempted to follow Franklin's route. They sailed through Lancaster Sound, the place where Franklin's ships had last been spotted. But a little further west in Peel Sound, ice conditions forced them to turn back. James Ross returned to England in 1849 without finding any signs of his old friend and the crew.

Sir John Richardson commanded another expedition in 1848. They planned to go overland through northwestern Canada. Richardson's party followed the Mackenzie River to the Arctic Ocean. From there, the expedition turned east and followed the coast to the mouth of the Coppermine River. Unfortunately, they also found no trace of Franklin. Richardson returned to England. John Rae, a member of the party, stayed in the Arctic to continue the search.

Though no sign of the expedition was found, Lady Jane did not give up hope. She was certain that her husband was still alive. She interviewed whaling captains for news. She wrote letters to world leaders, including President Zachary Taylor of the United States. Her determination made her a national heroine. The public pressured the Royal Navy to continue efforts to find and rescue the lost explorers.

By 1850, the search for Franklin was the largest rescue operation in history. That summer twelve ships headed for the North American Arctic region. Two were American expeditions. Lady Franklin even equipped and staffed a ship with her own money. They all planned to search the waterways north and west of Lancaster Sound.

Several rescue ships met near Beechey Island on the morning of August 27, 1850. Three of the captains were discussing where to look next. As they talked, a messenger arrived. "Graves, Captain Penny! Graves! Franklin's winter quarters," he shouted.[4] Dates on the graves showed that Franklin had spent his second

WITH A HUNDRED SEAMEN HE SAILED AWAY
TO THE FROZEN OCEAN IN THE MONTH OF MAY
TO SEEK A PASSAGE AROUND THE POLE
WHERE WE POOR SAILORS DO SOMETIMES GO.
THROUGH CRUEL HARDSHIPS THEY VAINLY STROVE
THEIR SHIPS ON MOUNTAINS OF ICE WERE DROVE
ONLY THE ESKIMO WITH HIS SKIN CANOE
WAS THE ONLY ONE THAT EVER CAME THROUGH
IN BAFFIN'S BAY WHERE THE WHALE FISH BLOW
THE FATE OF FRANKLIN NO MAN MAY KNOW
THE FATE OF FRANKLIN NO TONGUE CAN TELL
LORD FRANKLIN WITH HIS SAILORS DO DWELL.[5]

These verses are from "Lord Franklin," one of many poems and songs written in the mid-1800s about Sir John Franklin's lost expedition. The term Eskimo is not used today. The Inuit view the term as offensive.

winter here in 1846. But nothing had been left behind to indicate where Franklin planned to go from there.

The search continued in 1850 until heavy pack ice forced the ships south for the winter. New geographic discoveries were made and many new observations about the icy lands were noted. New adventures were recorded for history. However, no more information about the missing expedition was found.

Clues Uncovered

By 1853, hope of finding Franklin was dwindling. A few parties still explored the North American Arctic region looking for clues. That year John Rae (a member of Richardson's 1848 overland search for Franklin) set out on his fourth expedition in the region. He traveled overland from the northwest shores of Hudson Bay to the Great Fish River. From there, the expedition followed the river to the Arctic Ocean.

In April 1854, Rae met a group of Inuit hunters. They showed Rae silverware, coins, and other relics that could only have come from Franklin's ship. They told him a story about a group of thirty-five to forty white men. They had been spotted traveling south over the ice. They were dragging a small boat. None of the party spoke the Inuit language. By signs, the Inuit learned that the white men's ships had been crushed by ice. They all looked thin and had little food. The white men bought a small seal from the hunters.

Later that same season, Inuit had discovered thirty bodies a long day's journey northwest of Great Fish

The relics pictured were found with the bodies of Franklin's crew. In the center is a sextant, which is used for navigation. Above it is an oar that was used to paddle a canoe through the narrow Arctic channels. To the right of the sextant is a gun, which was used for hunting and protection.

River. Some of the bodies had been buried. Others were found in tents and under a boat, which had been turned over for shelter. The corpses had been mutilated. These starving men had been driven to cannibalism in hopes of surviving.[6] Rae quickly sent this information back to England.

Franklin's Final Fate

Rae's information left little hope of finding Franklin and his men alive. Public confidence in the Royal Navy dropped. Officials declared the commander and crew dead in 1854. Only Lady Jane refused to give up. Twelve years after Franklin first sailed, she used her own funds to send out a search party. Sir Francis Leopold McClintock led the expedition. During its first winter in 1857, McClintock met Inuit who told stories about two ships wrecked and crushed by ice. They also told stories about starving white men "who fell down and died as they walked along."[7]

McClintock sent out expeditions to search the area where these white men had been seen. They discovered a wood and iron sled loaded with a heavy ship's boat. The boat contained books, towels, soap, silver plates, shoes, watches, cigars, and two skeletons. McClintock also found two reports written by officers. The first was dated May 28, 1847. It stated that Franklin had sailed north up Wellington Channel and around Cornwallis Island. The party spent the winter of 1845–1846 on Beechey Island. The next summer the ships reached Peel Sound as far as the northern tip of

The ship's boat that Francis Leopold McClintock discovered held a grisly secret—two skeletons.

King William Island. Then they were trapped by ice. Franklin expected to complete the passage the next summer.

A second message written on April 25, 1848, was scribbled on the margin of the first. It painted a different picture. The ships had been trapped in ice for nineteen months. Twenty-four men had died, including Franklin. The survivors had decided to abandon ship and march overland to the mouth of the Great Fish River. They hoped to meet a rescue party there. Unfortunately, no one survived. No more records were found. The exact cause of Franklin's death had not been recorded. Many historians believe expedition members might have survived if they had known how to build igloos and hunt seal. However, it would have been very difficult for a party of more than one hundred men to live off the land in the Arctic.[8]

Franklin's downfall more likely was his faith in technology. He thought steam power and iron plating could overcome the Arctic pack ice. Unfortunately, steam engines were unreliable in frigid Arctic temperatures. When his ships became trapped by ice, the plating did not prevent them from being crushed. He depended on canned goods to keep his crew healthy and well. He expected to return home long before these supplies ran out. He made no back up plan to hunt or fish as the Inuit did for food. He also relied on modern instruments. These were to help his crew navigate unknown waters and find a passage free of ice.[9]

25TH APRIL 1848. H M SHIPS TERROR AND EREBUS WERE DESERTED ON THE 22ND APRIL 5 LEAGUES NNW OF THIS, HAVING BEEN BESET SINCE 12TH SEPR. 1846. THE OFFICERS AND CREWS CONSISTING OF 105 SOULS UNDER THE COMMAND OF CAPTAIN F.R.M. CROZIER LANDED HERE IN LAT. 69O 37' 42" LONG. 98O 41' . . . SIR JOHN FRANKLIN DIED ON THE 11TH OF JUNE 1847 AND THE TOTAL LOSS BY DEATHS IN THE EXPEDITION HAS BEEN TO THIS DATE 9 OFFICERS & 15 MEN. [SIGNED] JAMES FITZJAMES, CAPTAIN HMS EREBUS. F.R.M. CROZIER CAPTAIN & SENIOR OFFICER, AND START ON TOMORROW 26TH FOR BACKS FISH RIVER.[10]

McClintock found these two reports written on a British navy "bottle form." These forms were meant to be put into bottles and set afloat. This one painted a grim picture and left little hope of finding any survivors ten years after it had been written.

The weather stopped them. Extremely harsh winters kept channels frozen and impassable.

Even in death, Franklin served his country. The eleven-year search added to the knowledge about the North American Arctic region. And in fact, Franklin did find a Northwest Passage, though he was unable to navigate it because of ice. It proved to be one of several different routes discovered during the search for Sir John Franklin's lost expedition. Lady Jane now had the satisfaction of knowing that her husband accomplished what he set out to do. Franklin ended the search for the Northwest Passage.

The first explorers of the western hemisphere sailed north for one reason. They were looking for a much shorter, more dependable trade route from Europe to Cathay, as China was then called. They hoped to bring home shiploads of silk, gold, ivory, and unusual animals and plants from the east. At that time, Spain and Portugal controlled the southern sea routes. These routes took

SEARCH FOR A NEW TRADE ROUTE

ships around Africa's Cape of Good Hope or South America's Cape Horn. Both routes took many months and were dangerous to navigate.

Overland travel to China was also risky. The routes were often disrupted by wars in the Middle East. Bandits commonly attacked the caravans loaded with valuable goods as they headed home.

France and Great Britain decided to explore sea routes to the west and north. They hoped to find one that would make the trip to China shorter and easier. They had no idea that a huge landmass, the continent of North America, blocked their way. These early

John Cabot sailed across the North Atlantic with a crew of eighteen in the Mathew. *They were searching for a shorter route to China.*

explorers mapped large areas of new territory during their voyages. Unfortunately, no usable trade route was found.

A New World

The ships used by early explorers were small wooden vessels, powered by wind. Sailors had only a few simple tools to help them navigate uncharted regions. Even so, fearless captains set off in search of the Northwest Passage.

In May 1497, the Italian explorer John Cabot sailed with a crew of eighteen in the *Mathew* to search for a new western route to China. King Henry VII had granted the explorer the right for his expedition to sail under the English flag.

After thirty-five days at sea, the explorers sighted a rocky shoreline. The water was full of icebergs large enough to damage their small wooden ship. Cabot waited until morning to land. On shore, the sailors explored the thick forest within crossbow range of the ship (roughly one thousand feet). They found the remains of a campfire, a needle, snares (traps for game), and a long piece of wood painted red with a hole at each end. The crew refilled the ship's water barrels from a stream, then sailed south. Cabot worked his ship carefully along the shore of Newfoundland, located on the east coast of present-day Canada. He had to avoid rocky reefs and shallow water. They eventually sailed into an area where the sea seemed to overflow with codfish. Cabot's men could lower a weighted

I AM SENDING THE OTHER BOOK OF MARCO POLO AND A COPY OF THE LAND WHICH HAS BEEN FOUND [BY JOHN CABOT] . . . HE LANDED AT ONLY ONE SPOT OF THE MAINLAND, NEAR THE PLACE WHERE LAND WAS FIRST SIGHTED . . . IN THAT PARTICULAR SPOT . . . THEY FOUND A TRAIL THAT WENT INLAND, THEY SAW A SITE WHERE A FIRE HAD BEEN MADE, THEY SAW MANURE OF ANIMALS WHICH THEY THOUGHT TO BE FARM ANIMALS, AND THEY SAW A STICK HALF A YARD LONG PIERCED AT BOTH ENDS, CARVED AND PAINTED WITH BRAZIL, AND BY SUCH SIGNS THEY BELIEVED THE LAND TO BE INHABITED. SINCE HE WAS WITH JUST A FEW PEOPLE, HE DID NOT DARE ADVANCE INLAND BEYOND THE SHOOTING DISTANCE OF A CROSSBOW, AND AFTER TAKING IN FRESH WATER HE RETURNED TO HIS SHIP . . . [AS THEY SAILED ALONG THE] SHORE THEY SAW TWO FORMS RUNNING ON LAND ONE AFTER THE OTHER, BUT THEY COULD NOT TELL IF THEY WERE HUMAN BEINGS OR ANIMALS; AND IT SEEMED TO THEM THAT THERE WERE FIELDS WHERE THEY THOUGHT MIGHT ALSO BE VILLAGES. . . . THEY LEFT ENGLAND TOWARD THE END OF MAY, AND MUST HAVE BEEN ON THE WAY 35 DAYS BEFORE SIGHTING LAND.[1]

John Cabot's voyages were detailed in a letter written by an English merchant named John Day. He wrote this letter sometime between December 1497 and January 1498 to the "Lord Grand Admiral," probably Christopher Columbus.

basket into the water and pull it up filled with fish. The Europeans had discovered a fishing area now called the Grand Banks.

After cruising south for two weeks, the ship rounded Cape Race, the southeastern corner of Newfoundland. From there, the sea stretched west and south all the way to the horizon. Cabot was certain he had found the western sea route to China. He measured his latitude. He had reached 45 degrees, 45 minutes north.

Then the *Mathew* quickly returned to London. Cabot told his story to the king and proposed a second voyage. This time the explorer planned to sail further west, hugging the shore until he reached China and all its riches.

Cabot believed that the second voyage would take no more than fifteen days. He sailed from Bristol with a fleet of five ships in May 1498. Months passed with no word. It was as if Cabot had sailed, as superstitious sailors once believed, over the horizon and off the edge of the earth. Most likely Cabot and his ships sank during a storm on the Atlantic. However, his mysterious disappearance did not prevent others from searching for the Northwest Passage.

Explorers for France

Giovanni da Verrazzano, an Italian sailing for France, thought he would find a route to China somewhere along the North American coast between Florida and Newfoundland. He set sail on January 17, 1524, with two vessels, *La Dauphine* and *La Normande*. They soon met several Spanish ships. France and Spain were at war and Verrazzano captured the enemy ships. *Normande* went back to France with the captured ships. Verrazzano now had one ship and fifty men to complete the voyage. It was not considered safe for an expedition to sail across the Atlantic with only one ship, but Verrazzano decided to take the risk.

In March, *La Dauphine* reached a low-lying coast with sandy beaches and wide rolling dunes. Verrazzano recorded his latitude as 34 degrees north. It is likely he first sighted land just south of modern-day Cape Fear, North Carolina.

When the sailors spotted fires burning on the beach, Verrazzano sent men ashore in the ship's small rowboat. The American Indians were afraid of the strangers until the Frenchmen made signs to show they were friendly. Verrazzano described the people as dark in color. He noted their black hair, "which they tie together in a knot behind, and wear it like a tail." He said they went "altogether naked" except for wearing "skins of beasts around their loins."[2]

Verrazzano and his men explored the shore and then sailed north. After a few days, they spotted what the explorer called an "eastern sea." It was on the other side of a narrow peninsula. He was sure the route to China lay just over the barrier. Verrazzano searched for a way through, but could not find one. It is likely that his ship was sailing along the Outer Banks off Cape Hatteras, North Carolina. In this part of the coast, the land is barely a mile wide with ocean on both sides.

The company continued north, stopping sometimes to explore the shore. On April 17, they discovered "a very pleasant place situated amongst . . . little steep hills; from . . . the hills . . . a great stream of water" flowed out to sea.[3] This "stream" is known today as New York Bay.

Verrazzano continued his exploration until he reached the shores of Newfoundland. By then, the ship's supplies were nearly gone. *La Dauphine*'s crew loaded more wood and water aboard. They returned safely to France in July 1524.

After Verrazzano's thorough search of the North American coastline, future French and English explorers turned their attention further north. If a passage to China existed, it would be somewhere in those icy regions.

Ten years later, Jacques Cartier, another French explorer, sailed out to search for the Northwest Passage. Cartier had earned respect for his skills as a navigator and commander. He planned to look for a passage through the waterways west of Newfoundland. Cartier set sail with a crew of sixty-one in April 1534.

The two French ships reached Newfoundland on May 10. For the next ten days they were trapped in a harbor by ice and bad weather. Then they sailed west through the Strait of Belle Isle and along the rocky coast of southern Labrador.

Jacques Cartier was disappointed in Labrador. He described the area as a region where "little grass grows . . . but moss is plentiful. Mosquitoes and flies are troublesome in summer."[4]

On June 30, the ships approached a low coast with sandy beaches. The Frenchmen could see grassy meadows and tall trees in the distance. They made several brief landings along the beautiful coast, known today as Prince Edward Island. Cartier explored the region until August 1, but found no passage west. His officers and crew then voted to return to France. They did not want to spend the winter in a strange land.[5] The fleet reached France in September, about four and one half months after it had left.

In May 1535, Cartier left on a second voyage. When the three ships reached Newfoundland, a gale forced the fleet to shelter in a bay on the coast of Labrador north of Anticosti Island. Cartier named this bay the Gulf of St. Lawrence.

In early September, the ships discovered a river flowing into the gulf. Cartier named it La Grande Riviere, which means "large river" in French. Today, it is called the St. Lawrence River. The river flowed between high, stony hills, over dangerous shoals, and around several small islands. Cartier explored the river as far as present-day Montreal. At that point, rapids prevented his ships from sailing further upstream. He and his crew wintered along the river and returned to France in the summer of 1536.

Cartier made one more voyage in May 1541. He planned to settle the first French colony in the New World. The attempt failed and this ended French exploration for a Northwest Passage for more than fifty years.

The Days of Good Queen Bess

In 1558, Elizabeth Tudor, the twenty-five-year-old daughter of King Henry VIII became Queen Elizabeth I of England. Good Queen Bess, as her subjects called her, encouraged British exploration for a Northwest Passage.

In 1576, some London nobles hired Captain Martin Frobisher to lead an English expedition. His three ships were supplied with the latest books about navigation. These books included discoveries made by earlier explorers. Sailing into the Arctic region was no longer a complete mystery. The captain also took the most modern instruments. Using these tools, he hoped to locate the Northwest Passage.

SOURCE DOCUMENT

WHEN A FIELD [OF ICE] . . . BECOMES EXPOSED TO THE EFFECTS OF A . . . SWELL, IT PRESENTLY BREAKS INTO A GREAT MANY PIECES, FEW OF WHICH WILL EXCEED FORTY TO FIFTY YARDS IN DIAMETER. NOW, SUCH A NUMBER OF PIECES COLLECTED TOGETHER IN CLOSE CONTACT, SO THEY CANNOT, FROM THE TOP OF THE SHIP'S MAST, BE SEEN OVER ARE TERMED A *PACK*.[6]

William Scoresby, a British explorer, described Arctic ice conditions in his book The Polar Ice *in 1815.*

Frobisher sailed on June 7 with three vessels. His smallest ship sank in a storm in the North Atlantic. All hands were lost, but Frobisher continued west. On July 11, *The Gabriel* and *The Michael* sighted new land at latitude 61 degrees north. Thick ice pack near the mountainous coastline stopped them from reaching shore to explore. The icy conditions also frightened the captain and crew of *The Michael*. They raised their sails and made for home.

Frobisher and his eighteen remaining officers and crew decided to continue exploring. They sailed south along the coast and rounded the tip of what we now call Greenland. Turning northwest, *The Gabriel* sailed through open seas. The explorers spotted icebergs so massive they mistook them for land at first.

Near the end of July, the ship's lookout sighted land—Resolution Island. It is located nine hundred miles northwest of Newfoundland off the southeastern tip of Baffin Island. Ice again made a landing impossible.

On August 11, *The Gabriel* sailed northwest into a new waterway. Frobisher sailed one hundred fifty miles up the passage that he named Frobisher Strait. Today it is known as Frobisher Bay. On August 18, the explorers dropped anchor near an island in the passage. The next day, the captain and nine men rowed ashore in a small boat to search for inhabitants. From the top of the hill, they spotted floating objects. They thought these objects were porpoises, but the figures turned out to be fur-clad Inuit in kayaks. When the

Englishmen tried to trade with the Inuit, several sailors were taken captive.

Frobisher got even by single-handedly pulling an Inuk and his kayak onto *The Gabriel*'s deck. He planned to trade the captive for his sailors' release. However, by the next morning a foot of snow had fallen. With winter approaching, Frobisher decided to sail for England immediately. He took the "strange man" and his kayak along. The captive died in October 1576, a few days after the ship arrived in England. Most likely, he caught a cold during the voyage. Frobisher later made two more unsuccessful voyages into the Arctic region.

Frobisher sailed one hundred fifty miles up the passage that he named Frobisher Strait. Today, the body of water is known as Frobisher Bay.

The next English explorer was navigator John Davis. He was friendly, conscientious, and honest, and quickly gained the confidence of his men. He set sail in June 1585 with two small vessels.

Six weeks later, on July 19, the vessels entered a fog bank so thick that the crews lost sight of the other. The next day when the fog lifted, they saw a rocky, mountainous land—Greenland's east coast. The ships sailed around its southern tip and across a stretch of ocean now known as Davis Strait. The waterway is about one hundred fifty miles northeast of Frobisher Bay.

Arctic weather was mild that year. The ships were not stopped by heavy ice. This convinced Davis that a passage to China did exist. He returned to England in September certain he would find the passage on his next voyage. Davis made three more unsuccessful voyages, but he remained convinced the passage existed. Many others believed as he did and set out in small wooden ships to explore the ice-filled Arctic water.

B y the seventeenth century, sailing ships were larger and more of the coastline of North America had been charted. However, bigger ships and better maps did not make exploration safe. Sailing off in ships was only for the brave and bold of heart. Explorers' stories sometimes had a tragic end.

BRAVE EXPLORERS IN SMALL SHIPS

English navigator Henry Hudson made four attempts to find a passage through Arctic waterways. On his first expedition in 1607, he sailed nearer the North Pole than anyone ever had. Hudson tried again the following year. He rounded the northern tip of Norway and discovered that the sun shone twenty-four hours a day during the Arctic summer. He sighted large numbers of whales off the west coast of Spitsbergen. The information he brought back started an Arctic whaling industry, but Hudson failed to find a passage. Weather forced his ship south during a third voyage. Hudson ended up along the coast of present-day New England and explored a river that now bears his name, the

Hudson. He also explored the coast of present-day New Jersey.

In April 1610, Hudson left England on his final voyage. As his ship, the *Discovery*, sailed northwest the weather and seas grew dangerous. His crew threatened mutiny, but Hudson refused to turn back. *Discovery* forced its way through an icy passage, now named Hudson Strait, that separates northern Labrador from Baffin Island.

In August, Hudson sighted a body of water so big he was sure that it must be the Pacific Ocean. What he had actually discovered was a huge bay now named after him. Hudson Bay, ice-covered nine months of the year, proved to be an icy trap instead of the passage he was looking for.

For the next two months, the *Discovery* followed the coastline southward some six hundred miles, only to find it was a dead end. Winter was coming, but Hudson spent several more weeks sailing back and forth across the bay. As the crew explored, the bay began to freeze.

By November 1610, the *Discovery* was trapped. It was a hard, cold winter and many of Hudson's crew became ill. Food supplies ran short. The sailors survived by catching a few birds and fish. Hudson accused the crew of hoarding food and searched their sea chests. The sailors suspected that Hudson was the one secreting rations away.[1]

When the ice melted the following spring, the ship's crew wanted to return home, but the captain

The last voyage Henry Hudson made was in a small wooden boat. Angry crewmembers abandoned Hudson, his son, and sailors who were loyal to the explorer on Hudson Bay. Hudson and his party were never seen again.

ordered them to sail west. By June 1611, angry crew members forced Hudson, his son, and sailors who were loyal to the explorer or who were ill into a small boat and abandoned them. A handful of sailors made it back to England aboard the *Discovery*. They were tried but not punished. Hudson and the others were never heard from again.

New Discoveries on the Arctic Map

Many hoped that the great bay Hudson had discovered would lead to a passage to China. In 1615, Commander Robert Bylot and English navigator William Baffin took the *Discovery* northwest again. They searched for a waterway leading out of the bay. Instead, the explorers found that the water at the bay's north end was blocked by ice. Along the way, Baffin made many observations and kept careful records. His maps were very accurate.[2] Later explorers used them to navigate the bay.

Back in England, Baffin reported that if a passage existed through the Hudson Bay, it was "but some creeke or inlet."[3] He suggested that future searches be made in the open sea beyond Davis Strait.

The next spring, Bylot and Baffin sailed again. This voyage would later be recognized as one of the most fruitful in the history of maritime discovery.[4] They rounded the south end of Greenland and pushed up Davis Strait. By the end of May, they reached Davis' furthest point and entered new territory. These two explorers sailed beyond 78 degrees latitude. They traveled three hundred miles farther north than any explorer before them. It was a record that stood for more than two centuries. Baffin also mapped the bay that now bears his name.

During this voyage, Bylot and Baffin found three broad openings. They named them Lancaster, Jones, and Smith sounds. These deep sounds would prove to be important waterways during future exploration. In fact, Smith Sound was the gateway to the North Pole. Unfortunately, Baffin thought that the ice-choked sounds were merely inlets that led nowhere. "Here our hope of a passage began to lessen every day," he recorded.[5] Although Bylot and Baffin failed to find the Northwest Passage, their explorations added important details to the Arctic map.

SOURCE DOCUMENT

"THERE IS NO PASSAGE NOR HOPE OF PASSAGE IN THE NORTH OF DAVIS STREIGHTS, WEE HAVING COASTED ALL OR NEERE ALL THE CIRCUMFERENCE THEREOF, AND FINDE IT TO BE NO OTHER THAN A GREAT BAY."[6]

William Baffin recorded this statement after his final voyage. His judgment was accepted as fact. For many decades, explorers ignored Davis Strait and Lancaster, Jones, and Smith sounds as they searched for the Northwest Passage.

Passage From the Pacific

Captain James Cook led the next British expedition in search of the Northwest Passage. His quest would start from the Pacific side of the Arctic Ocean. The Captain sailed from England in July 1776. He sailed around South America's Cape Horn with his two ships, *Resolution* and *Discovery*. It was a long voyage. (Cook had already made two voyages to the southern hemisphere.) He planned to reach the North American coast sometime in June 1777. Unfortunately, his ships were in poor condition. He had to stop often on islands in the South Pacific to make repairs.

By November 1777, *Resolution* and *Discovery* were repaired and ready to sail. In an unexplored section of the North Pacific, the expedition discovered a group of islands. Cook named them the Sandwich Islands, in honor of the Earl of Sandwich. He was the commander of the British Royal Navy. (Today we know these islands as the state of Hawaii.)

The ships finally sighted the northwest coast of America on March 7, 1778. Cook again had to search for a safe harbor. Two masts on *Resolution* needed to be replaced. Near the end of April, the ships prepared to sail north. Their holds were filled with skins, mostly sea otter pelts. They had traded for the valuable furs with the Nootka tribe that lived along the coast of present-day Canada and Washington State.

Cook now sailed steadily north from the west coast of Vancouver Island. He followed orders: ". . . not to lose any time in exploring rivers or inlets, or upon any

Near the end of April, Captain James Cook's ships prepared to sail north. Their holds were filled with skins, mostly sea otter pelts. They had traded for the valuable furs with the Nootka tribe that lived along the coast of present day Canada and Washington State.

other account, until you get into the . . . latitude of 65 degrees north."[7]

Along his route, the captain named places still found on modern maps—Cape Edgecumbe, Cross Sound, and Cape Fairweather. For several weeks, the expedition sailed in and out of wide waterways. All turned out to be dead ends. During this time, they explored Prince William Sound and Cook Inlet near present-day Anchorage, Alaska.

By early June, Cook seemed headed in the wrong direction. The ships had to sail southwest along the long tongue of the Alaskan peninsula. Finally, they rounded its end and sailed northeast, only to be disappointed again. Instead of a Northwest Passage, Cook had discovered another large inlet, Bristol Bay. His ships had to backtrack nearly two hundred miles west to reach open sea and head north toward the Bering Strait.

On August 9, the expedition sighted the western tip of the North American continent. Cook named it Cape Prince of Wales. For a few days, the ships made steady progress northeast. Then Cook wrote: "Some time before noon we perceived a brightness in the Northern horizon like that reflected from ice, commonly called the blink . . . At 1 P.M. the sight of a large field of ice left us no longer in doubt about the cause of the brightness . . ."[8] They had reached latitude

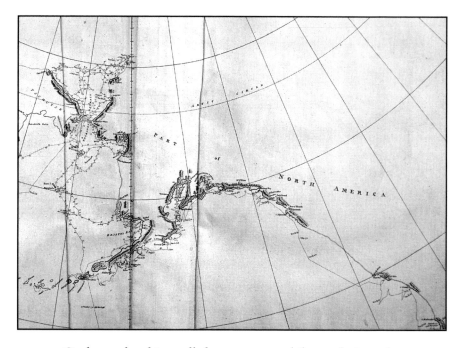

Cook made this well-drawn map while exploring the northwestern coast of North America. It was the first accurate representation of the region.

70 degrees 45 minutes north, but could go no further. The ice blocked their way. It extended east and west as far as they could see.

Alarmed by the steady drift of the pack ice southward, Cook retreated. He did not want his ships crushed between the shore and the oncoming ice.[9] The *Resolution* and *Discovery* followed the edge of ice east toward the coast of Asia, but found no passage through. Near the end of August, snow and fog announced winter's arrival. Cook decided to return to the islands he had discovered. There he could winter comfortably and prepare for another voyage to the Alaskan Arctic the next summer.

The ships landed in Hawaii in January. During their stay on the island, relations between the Englishmen and the Hawaiians deteriorated. Cook ignored the growing hostility until one of the ship's rowboats was stolen. He went ashore on February 14, 1778, to recover the boat. A fight broke out between the crew and the Hawaiians. Cook was killed in the scuffle. Their captain's death distressed the crew. "Everyone in the ships was stricken dumb, crushed, and felt as though he had lost his father," one sailor recorded.[10]

The ships left the Hawaiian Islands in the middle of March. They sailed back to the Bering Strait, following the earlier orders of their dead captain. On July 6, they reached latitude 67 degrees north and again encountered a wall of ice. The two ships made repeated attempts to get through the drift ice, but could not

Captain James Cook and his men were served roast pig by the people of the Sandwich Islands (today, Hawaii).

find a passage. The *Discovery* was badly battered by ice. The two ships put into a nearby port for repairs, and then set sail for the long voyage home.

The ships arrived in England in October 1780, more than four years after they had begun their voyage. Cook's officers brought home charts he had made during the voyage. The charts were published in 1784. They were Cook's lasting legacy to exploration. For the first time, the shape of the northwestern coast of North America was accurately mapped. The continent's outline was not what Cook had expected to find. English mapmakers, men who had never sailed the

Pacific Ocean, had drawn maps and charts of the area based on theory. These charts were wrong. It had made navigation through the region difficult. Cook's careful records assisted others who followed his lead to the northwest. With this new knowledge, explorers could now navigate confidently through the waters off the Alaskan coast.

4

SIR JOHN BARROW'S PUSH FOR ARCTIC EXPLORATION

The search for the Northwest Passage was interrupted for nearly thirty years by wars in Europe. To fight these wars, Great Britain built a huge navy. In 1815, when the wars were over, all these ships and men had very little to do. John Barrow, the second secretary of the admiralty, suggested that they explore the Arctic regions—searching for the Northwest Passage. The British Parliament agreed and offered rewards to encourage exploration.

Over the next forty years, British expeditions charted large coastal areas of Greenland. They explored many islands in the icy waterways near Canada, and most of the Arctic coastline of North America. They also collected data about temperatures, ice conditions, and life in the Arctic region.

The English Discover the "Arctic Highlanders"

John Ross had joined the Royal Navy when he was only nine and fought during the Napoleonic War. Ross was now forty-one and a captain. He was chosen to lead the first British expedition in search of a northwest passage after the war. His second-in-command was William Edward Parry. They sailed on April 21, 1818, in *Isabella* and *Alexander*. Ross believed both vessels were unfit for the voyage, but the Navy refused to build special vessels for Arctic exploration. Instead, the Navy reinforced the ships' hulls to help them battle the ice.

By mid-June, the expedition entered Davis Strait and sailed north along the coast of Greenland. The officers and crews had their first view of the icy sea. They were amazed by its strangeness. Ross wrote: "It is hardly possible to imagine anything more exquisite . . . by night as well as by day they glitter with a vividness of colour beyond the power of art to represent. . . ."[1]

On July 2, the two ships sailed into a sea of icebergs. Sailing grew more and more dangerous. Fog blinded the crews. During a gale, the sterns of the *Isabella* and the *Alexander* smashed together. Both the ships and their lifeboats were damaged, but still able to sail.

A day or so later the expedition made an important discovery. Ross and Parry came face-to-face with an unknown group of Inuit, not far from the village of Etah. Even Ross's interpreter from South Greenland had never heard of them before. Ross named them the "Arctic Highlanders."

The Inuit on the shore were clearly afraid of the English ships. One officer marched forward with a white flag decorated with a sign that symbolized

John Ross and William Edward Parry came face to face with an unknown group of Inuit. Ross named them the "Arctic Highlanders."

peace—a hand holding an olive branch. This meant nothing to the people of this treeless land. Ross finally put a flag on a pole and tied a bag full of presents to it. The group understood that the gifts were a sign of friendship and peace.

These Inuit had had no contact with the world beyond their shores. They were sure the men with sickly looking skins came from the sky. They had never seen a boat, not even a kayak. They thought the English ships were alive. "We have seen them move their wings," they said, referring to the ships' sails.[2]

Other things surprised the Inuit. They looked for a monster hiding behind a mirror. They tasted biscuits and spit them out in disgust. They asked what kind of ice the windowpanes were made of and what kind of animal produced the strange "skins" the officers were wearing. They thought a watch was alive and asked if it was good to eat. A little pig frightened them. They enjoyed watching a crew member use a hammer and nails. The ship's wooden furniture puzzled them. The largest tree that grew on these icy shores was a dwarf shrub with a stem no thicker than a finger.

Without investigating how these people survived in their frozen Arctic home, Ross, Parry, and their men sailed north again. Along the way, they studied currents and tides. They made notes about the ice conditions. They also collected Arctic plant and animal specimens.

The *Isabella* and the *Alexander* soon reached the top of Baffin Bay. From there, the ships sailed west to the southern tip of what is now Ellesmere Island, then south. Near the end of August, the expedition reached Lancaster Sound.

After sailing up the foggy sound some thirty miles due west, Ross spotted what he believed to be a chain of high mountains blocking their route. What Ross probably saw was an Arctic mirage, or illusion. He added the Croker Mountains to his chart then, without a word to Parry, turned about and headed for home. A member of the *Alexander*'s crew recorded the disappointment felt aboard ship. "Thus vanished our golden dreams, our brilliant hopes, our high expectations!"[3] Parry and most of the crew expected to winter in the Arctic region if they did not find the passage that first year. The expedition was supplied with winter clothing and provisions for another season.

The two ships returned to England on November 11, 1818. Ross had discovered a new band of Inuit, made scientific observations, and collected new botanical specimens. He wrote a report that included three folding charts. On one of these charts, he indicated that Lancaster Sound was a dead end—blocked to the west by a range of mountains—and could not possibly lead to a Northwest Passage.

Through the "Croker Mountains"

Secretary Barrow was disappointed that Ross's expedition had failed to find the Northwest Passage. He immediately made plans to expand the search. The following spring two expeditions were sent out.

Barrow selected William Edward Parry, Ross's second-in-command, to lead the sea expedition. Parry was only twenty-eight-years-old and felt lucky to be chosen. John Franklin led the other expedition. Franklin was to travel overland through the Canadian Arctic region and explore the coastline of North America. Barrow believed that one of these two groups would discover the Northwest Passage for the glory of England.

As Parry prepared to sail, he considered the problems Arctic explorers faced. His biggest concern was scurvy, a disease caused by not having enough vitamin C in the diet. He asked that juice for the voyage be prepared from fresh lemons. He also ordered canned soup, vegetables, and meats. Canning to preserve food had just been invented. It was so new, in fact, that no one had invented a can opener. Parry's cooks had to use an ax to open the cans. Parry believed these foods would keep his crew healthier.

The young captain also made plans to deal with boredom during the long Arctic winter. For eight months or more, his crew would be imprisoned inside the ship. Living so close together with little to do, sailors grew restless. Parry planned to keep his men busy. There would be music, sports, theatricals, and a newspaper to be printed. Parry even loaded a barrel organ aboard.

On May 11, 1819, Parry's ships, the *Griper* and the *Hecla*, sailed. They crossed the Atlantic and headed up Davis Strait. By the first of August, Parry entered Lancaster Sound and soon sailed through Ross's imaginary mountains. The crew of the *Griper* shouted their congratulations to Parry for his "escape from Croker's Mountains."[4]

From here, the expedition sailed west along what is now called Parry Channel. The explorer added more names to the Arctic map: Devons Island, Wellington Channel, Cornwallis and Bathurst Islands, and Viscount Melville Sound.

On September 4, the *Griper* and the *Hecla* crossed longitude 110 degrees west. Parry announced that they had earned the five-thousand-pound reward offered by Parliament. "It was a proud moment for us," wrote the purser, "it at once compensated for all the misery and

In 1819, William Edward Parry crossed the Atlantic and headed up Davis Strait. By the first of August, his ships entered Lancaster Sound and soon sailed through Ross's imaginary mountains.

mortification of the last voyage."[5] In only five weeks, Parry had explored some eight hundred miles of new coastline.

By the end of September, the weather grew cold and ice formed in the channels. Parry decided to set up winter quarters in Winter Harbour on the south shore of Melville Island. He organized a daily schedule to keep his crew busy. The men were up before six, scrubbing the decks with warm sand. Breakfast was served at eight. Parry inspected his crew at nine, and then everyone ran on the deck or on shore if the weather permitted. Afternoons were spent drawing, knotting yarn, and making repairs. After supper, games, singing, and dancing filled the hours until bedtime at nine.

Parry was not prepared though for the Arctic cold. Things that worked fine in England failed in below freezing conditions. Touching a bare hand on metal and trying to remove it tore off the skin. A telescope placed against the eye burned like a branding iron. Lemon juice and vinegar froze solid, breaking containers. Even the mercury in the thermometers froze. The men's leather boots froze hard and did not protect toes from frostbite. Parry devised better footwear from canvas and animal hides.

No amount of fuel could keep the ships warm when temperatures dropped far below zero. Officers played chess bundled up in scarves and great coats. Though the crews were never warm, they still managed to produce and print a weekly newspaper and put on theatricals.

Even with all Parry's precautions, by the middle of March ten men were sick from scurvy. In April, temperatures gradually warmed to a chilly 32 degrees Fahrenheit. Ptarmigan, caribou, and other game migrated back to the area in early May. It was thought that fresh meat reduced health problems, but it came too late for one seaman who died from scurvy. (Those who suffer from scurvy actually benefit from a diet of fresh vegetables and citrus fruits.)

In June, Parry traveled north across Melville Island on a two-week trek. The twelve men in the party dragged eight hundred pounds of equipment that had been loaded on a two-wheeled cart. This was the first attempt to man-haul gear on an overland expedition. On the other side of the island, Parry found a huge natural harbor. He named it Hecla and Griper Bay.

Ice still choked the harbor in July as the men prepared the ships to sail. It was not until August 4 that the *Griper* and the *Hecla* could sail west again. All winter Parry had planned to depart from Winter Harbour and sail quickly on to the Bering Sea. Luck was not with him this season. Ice blocked his route everywhere that the ships went.

On August 23, 1820, Parry reached Cape Providence on the west side of Melville Island. He said that the six miles covered that day were "the most difficult navigation [he] had ever known among ice."[6] British warships were bigger and stronger than ships

FOR THE WINTER CHRONICLE.
I SAT ME DOWN WITH FIRM INTENT
TO WRITE FOR THE GAZETTE,
BUT SOON THE COLD MY FINGERS BENT,
AND MADE ME FUME AND FRET,
MY GREAT COAT THEN I BUTTON'S UP,
PUT MY NIGHT-CAP ON MY HEAD,
OF COFFEE TOOK ANOTHER CUP,
AND ATE SOME TOASTED BREAD. . . .

MY FINGERS STILL WERE COLD AS LEAD,
MY TOES WITH PAIN WERE SMARTING,
MY TEETH KEPT CHATTERING IN MY HEAD,
AND LIFE SEEM'D FAST DEPARTING.
WHEN, NOTWITHSTANDING THIS SAD PLIGHT,
MY SUBJECT I HAD CHOSEN,
PRODUCED MY PAPER FAIR AND WHITE,
BEHOLD! MY INK WAS FROZEN![7]

This is a selection from a poem published in the ship newspaper the "Winter Chronicle." It was written to entertain and keep Parry's men's spirits high during the long boring winter months.

used by earlier explorers. Unfortunately, they were still no match for the Arctic pack ice.

Now, Parry realized the expedition would not reach the Bering Sea that year. Reluctantly, he turned his ships eastward. For a while, he looked for another route to the south, but with no luck. At the end of August, he sailed for England. *Griper* and *Hecla* reached home near the end of October 1820 with all but one of the ninety-four men who had gone north under Parry's command.

This experience convinced Parry that the route through Lancaster Sound was impassable. A different route needed to be found. He suggested that future explorers hug the North American coastline, the territory that was being explored that same winter by John Franklin and his overland expedition.

Parry sailed off to the Arctic in ships outfitted with the best the Royal Navy could supply. He took canned soups, vegetables, and meats. He also packed books, a printing press, and instruments to prevent boredom. At this same time, John Franklin prepared for an overland expedition. His list of supplies was much shorter. His party had to pack everything they needed in small canoes or on sleds.

OVERLAND SEARCH FOR THE NORTHWEST PASSAGE

Franklin, Dr. John Richardson, George Back, Robert Hood, and John Hepburn left England in May 1818 with a crew of four Scottish seamen. In two ships, they sailed across the Atlantic, through Hudson Strait, and across Hudson Bay. Their destination was the trading post at York Factory. Two Canadian trading companies had agreed to help Franklin. They supplied the clothing, ammunition, snowshoes, and food that would be needed. They also suggested the best route through the wilderness to the coast.

Franklin relied on the Canadians' advice. They knew best the dangers in traveling across this territory. In winter, the rivers froze solid. The sun did not shine for weeks. Temperatures dropped far below zero. There were few roads or trails—and fewer trading posts to restock food supplies. Franklin hoped to avoid many problems by hiring expert boatmen, guides, and hunters for his expedition.

His task was to chart the coast east and west of the Coppermine and Mackenzie rivers in Northwestern Canada. In addition, Franklin was expected to record data about temperature, wind, the aurora borealis (northern lights), and geomagnetism. The expedition was also to bring back detailed sketches of the land and its people.

The Journey Begins

Franklin's party left York Factory on September 13, 1819. The first part of the journey was made in river freighters. These lightweight boats were about forty feet long. Freighters were easily rowed across lakes and down streams, but it took a crew of nine to twelve to travel upriver. The boats had to be pulled by boatmen walking along shore on a trail. They took turns, but it was tiring work. Franklin and his officers walked along behind the boatmen, sometimes stumbling over fallen logs or slipping on wet rocks.

They fished and hunted as they traveled. After setting up camp and eating their evening meal, the officers checked maps, records, and equipment. Then everyone crawled under buffalo robes to sleep. Near the end of the month, they woke to find snow covering their robes. The weather grew colder, but they kept going. They paddled and pulled. Sometimes they had to unload the boats and carry everything around rapids and falls.

On October 23, they arrived at Cumberland House, a Hudson's Bay Company trading post on the Saskatchewan River. They had covered seven hundred miles since leaving York Factory. The river froze soon after they arrived. Traveling further by water was now impossible until spring.

Franklin needed to hire hunters, guides, and interpreters for the next leg of his trip. There were none at Cumberland House. He decided to hike nearly nine hundred miles to Fort Chipewyan on Lake Athabasca to find the help he needed. Franklin left Dr. Richardson and Hood at Cumberland House. The doctor wanted to study the customs of the friendly Cree Indians who lived near the post.

A Winter Trek

On January 19, 1820, Franklin, Back, and Hepburn set off on foot. Their equipment was loaded on dog sleds. The men wore snowshoes that were nearly six feet long and one-and-a-half feet wide. Each shoe weighed two pounds when free of snow. Walking all day in this special gear often left blisters on the men's feet. Franklin said later that walking in snowshoes was one of the worst parts of this trip.

They covered 857 miles in two months and arrived at Fort Chipewyan on March 26. Franklin immediately asked what the territory was like to the north. The company agent replied, "Snow. Ice. Barren ground. Eskimo country. No one goes there."[1]

On to Winter River

Dr. Richardson and Hood arrived at Fort Chipewyan on July 13 after the rivers thawed. They brought all the supplies that Cumberland House could provide. By July 18, Franklin's party was on the move again. They left Fort Chipewyan in canoes paddled by Canadian *voyageurs* (boatmen). Ten days later, they arrived at Fort Providence on the north shore of Great Slave Lake. Here they hired American Indian hunters. They would keep the expedition supplied with food on the journey. By this time, expeditions often depended on Inuit support as they lived and worked in Arctic conditions.

Fort Providence was the last post before plunging into unknown territory. Franklin and his men gathered all the flour, moose meat, pemmican or dried meat, chocolate, reindeer tongues, and tea the trading post could spare. Even then, Franklin worried that it would not be enough. They also took gifts for the American Indians—blankets, needles, mirrors, beads, and fishing nets.

The expedition now included Franklin, his officers, a trading company clerk, seventeen boatmen, and three interpreters. Three of the boatmen's wives also went

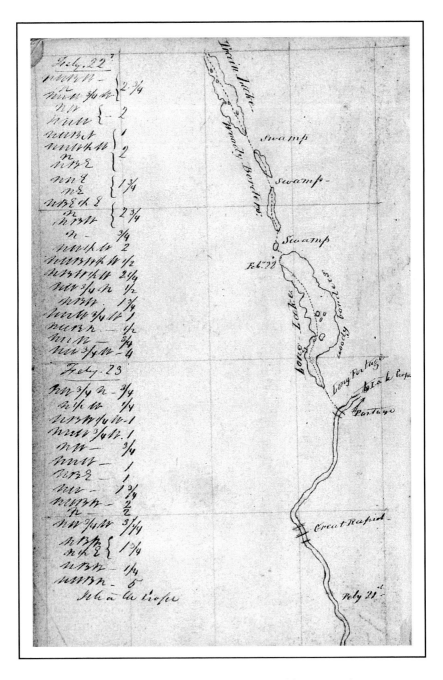

George Back drew this map during Franklin's expedition.

along. They would make shoes and clothes for the men once a winter post was built.

The group arrived at Winter River on August 20— a place chosen by their guides for the winter quarters. It was too late to set out for the Arctic Ocean this season, but Franklin, Dr. Richardson, and two others walked to the Coppermine River.

While Franklin's party was gone, the others started building a winter home. The shelter was completed by early October. It was a log building, fifty feet long and twenty-four feet wide. It was divided into a hall, three bedrooms, and a kitchen. The walls were plastered with clay. The floor was covered with rough planks and the windows were closed with deerskin parchment. Franklin named their camp Fort Enterprise.

George Back sketched Fort Chipewyan, one of the stops for Franklin's overland expedition.

To explore the rivers of Arctic Canada, John Franklin traveled in small boats like the ones in this picture.

During the winter, the men built two canoes for the expedition. Supplies grew short, as Franklin had feared. The hunters were not reliable. When a family member died, they refused to hunt until they were done mourning. The Englishmen had a difficult time understanding this custom, especially when food supplies ran low. In the middle of winter, Back and a small party trekked more than eleven hundred miles on snowshoes to Fort Chipewyan.[2] They went to see why they had not received more supplies. Back returned in March with some supplies and the promise of more.

During the winter, temperatures dropped to 57 degrees below zero outside and 40 below inside. To keep busy, the men played games, sang, and danced. Sometimes they made candles and soap or gathered wood. They hiked along the river and sledded down the hills. Charts were corrected and descriptions of the region written. Now and then a few supplies arrived, but never enough to allow the party more than a single meal a day.

Down the Coppermine to the Coast

On June 14, 1821, Franklin's party left for the Coppermine River and the Arctic Sea. He was worried about starting off with so few provisions. The expedition would have to live off the land, and their ammunition supply was short.

Several boatmen and two Inuit interpreters accompanied Franklin and his officers. Hunters were left behind to be sure that food supplies were replenished at Fort Enterprise by September, in case the party returned by that route. The women were sent home.

The expedition reached the mouth of the Coppermine a week after leaving the fort. From there, they traveled east for over five hundred miles. They explored the rocky, icy coast in two birch-bark canoes, charting Coronation Gulf, Bathurst Inlet, and more.

By August 22, John Franklin realized they could go no further. It was time to head back. Retracing their route would take too long, so Franklin decided to go overland to Fort Enterprise.

The Men Who Ate Their Shoes

They headed south from Point Turnagain at the east end of Coronation Gulf. Every day the weather grew colder. Snow fell and made breaking a trail difficult. Rivers often blocked their path. Franklin and his men looked for narrow places they could cross by hopping from rock to rock. Unfortunately, the rocks were slippery. Sometimes they fell into the icy water. In fact, Franklin nearly drowned while crossing one stream. He lost his journal and all the notes he had made on the expedition.

Food ran out as they struggled on. Sometimes the men gathered lichen off rocks, killed a partridge, or found berries to eat. Once they even ate a rotten deer carcass. Sometimes they just went hungry. In early October, Franklin recorded that the whole party ate what was left of their old moccasins and any scraps of leather they had.

By now, every man was exhausted. They began to leave instruments, books, and equipment behind. It was all they could do to walk. Franklin realized something had to be done. He sent Back and four of the strongest men on ahead to get help. He planned to keep the others together and get back to Fort Enterprise where a supply of food would be waiting.

However, later that day it became obvious that several men were too weak to continue. Franklin reluctantly agreed to go on without them. For thousands of Arctic miles he had kept his men together. Now, he had to leave the sick and weak behind. He

SOURCE DOCUMENT

THE DISTANCE WALKED TO-DAY WAS SIX MILES. . . .
PREVIOUS TO SETTING OUT, THE WHOLE PARTY ATE THE
REMAINS OF THEIR OLD SHOES, AND WHATEVER SCRAPS OF
LEATHER THEY HAD, TO STRENGTHEN THEIR STOMACHS FOR
THE FATIGUE OF THE DAY'S JOURNEY. WE LEFT
ENCAMPMENT AT NINE, AND PURSUED OUR ROUTE OVER A
RANGE OF BLEAK HILLS. THE WIND HAVING INCREASED TO A
STRONG GALE . . . BECAME PIERCINGLY COLD, AND THE DRIFT
. . . [MADE] IT DIFFICULT FOR THOSE IN THE REAR TO
FOLLOW THE TRACK OVER THE HEIGHTS . . . THE STOUTEST
MEN OF THE PARTY NOW EARNESTLY URGED . . . ME TO
ALLOW THEM TO THROW DOWN THEIR LOADS AND PROCEED
TO FORT ENTERPRIZE WITH THE UTMOST SPEED . . . MR.
HOOD AND DR. RICHARDSON PROPOSED TO REMAIN BEHIND
. . . AND I SHOULD PROCEED AS EXPEDITIOUSLY [QUICKLY] AS
POSSIBLE WITH THE MEN TO THE HOUSE, AND THENCE SEND
THEM IMMEDIATE RELIEF. THEY STRONGLY URGED THAT
THIS ARRANGEMENT WOULD CONTRIBUTE TO THE SAFETY OF
THE REST OF THE PARTY, BY RELIEVING THEM FROM THE
BURDEN OF A TENT AND SEVERAL OTHER ARTICLES . . . I WAS
DISTRESSED BEYOND DESCRIPTION AT THE THOUGHT OF
LEAVING THEM IN SUCH A DANGEROUS SITUATION . . . BUT I
RELUCTANTLY AGREED TO IT.[3]

*Franklin's expedition charted an impressive three
hundred fifty miles of the Canadian coast, but on the
return trip eleven men were lost before help arrived.
Franklin recorded these thoughts when he had to leave
several members of the party behind.*

wrote: "There was, however, no alternative . . . The party was now reduced to five . . . [including] myself."[4]

One Last Hope

Franklin's party reached Fort Enterprise the next afternoon. They hoped to gather supplies and return to the others. But the fort was deserted. The food they expected to find had not been sent. Instead, Franklin found a note from Back. He had left two days before. He was going for help.

The whole party wept for their friends.[5] Franklin knew the men who had been left behind could not last much longer without food and shelter. But all he could do was wait and hope Back returned quickly.

A few days later, Dr. Richardson and Hepburn reached the fort. They had been with those who stayed behind. The doctor reported that Hood and everyone else had died.

On November 7, the four surviving members of Franklin's expedition heard a gunshot. Help had finally arrived. Back had sent a rescue party with food—some dried deer meat. After eating and regaining their strength, the survivors left Fort Enterprise on November 16, 1821. "And thus terminated," wrote Franklin, "our long, fatiguing, and disastrous travels in North America."[6]

Franklin Returns

Franklin made a second trip to the Canadian Arctic in 1825. He had learned from mistakes made during his first expedition and had none of the same problems. He built better boats and started his return trip earlier to avoid being caught by winter weather. He also made sure the group was well supplied with food.

This time Franklin led his expedition up the Mackenzie River to the Arctic Coast. Here the group divided into two parties. Franklin followed the coast west exploring 374 miles of unknown territory along the Canadian and Alaskan coasts.

Dr. Richardson, Franklin's second-in-command, traveled east. He explored from the mouth of the Mackenzie to the Coppermine River, navigating 863 miles of Canadian coastline.

In 1827, Franklin and Richardson returned to England, proud of what they had accomplished. Together, they had added significant information to the Arctic map. A decade would pass before anyone would complete the work Franklin began and fill in the missing pieces of the North American coastline.

As more explorers sailed north, they relied on what was then modern equipment to tame the Arctic. In 1828, Captain John Ross planned another attempt to find a passage. This time he decided to see if modern technology—a steamship—could overcome the pack ice. The British Royal Navy turned the captain down. They questioned his dependability. On his first voyage, Ross had turned back after "seeing" mountains that appeared to block Lancaster Sound. Parry later proved these mountains did not exist.

FOUR ARCTIC WINTERS

Ross finally persuaded an old friend to finance the voyage. Naval Commander James Clark Ross, the captain's nephew, agreed to go as his second-in-command. Ross bought a paddle steamer, the *Victory*, for this Arctic voyage. He fitted her with new paddles that could be hoisted out of the water in a minute. This would prevent the paddles from being damaged by ice. Ross also modified the steam engines.

The expedition departed in May 1829 and ran into stormy weather while steaming across the North

Atlantic. The new engines proved to be unreliable, even in waters not packed with ice. When they reached port in Greenland, Ross had the crew rig the *Victory* for sailing. They used the masts and sails from an abandoned whaler. He also purchased more provisions and six husky dogs before sailing north.

By early August, the *Victory* had crossed Baffin Bay and entered Lancaster Sound. The weather was mild and the ship ran into very little ice until it entered Prince Regent Inlet. Ross landed briefly at Fury Beach. Parry's last expedition had lost a ship on this point and had left a cache of supplies and several small boats. Polar bears had destroyed the canvas tents Parry had abandoned, but tins of preserved meat and vegetables, wine, sugar, bread, and cocoa were undamaged.

For the next several weeks, *Victory* sailed south along the coast of the Boothia Peninsula, exploring a huge bay Ross named the Gulf of Boothia.

The First Winter

By early October, the expedition needed to prepare for winter. They found a safe bay for the *Victory* and named it Felix Harbour. The crew used blocks of snow to build a wall around the ship. Sails were stretched over the vessel to make a roof. Ross had his crew dismantle the steam engines and dumped them on the shore. They were taking up too much space and there were no plans to use them again. The new technology did not work well in cold Arctic temperatures.

On January 9, 1830, a party of thirty Inuit approached the *Victory*. James Clark Ross, who spoke some of the Inuit language, established friendly relations with the group. He invited two or three to come aboard. Later the Englishmen visited the Inuit village. About one hundred people lived in eighteen snow huts. After this first visit, the Inuit communicated and traded daily with Ross's crew. Due to racial attitudes of the time, officers were wary of the Inuit at first. They expected them to steal and cheat. Instead, the Englishmen were surprised by their honesty. Sometimes there were thefts. However, the Inuit seemed to think it a huge joke when they were caught.[1]

During the first winter, the younger Ross made several treks by dog sled. He wanted to learn as much as possible about the area's geography. He sledded across an ice-covered waterway, now called James Ross Strait, west of the Boothia Peninsula and discovered King William's Land on the other side.

In April, as James Clark Ross set out on another journey, a serious problem developed between the Inuit and English explorers. A falling stone had killed a boy. The Inuit were superstitious. They thought his death was caused by witchcraft and believed the Englishmen were responsible. Ross faced off against the angry Inuit as they threatened him with drawn knives. Through careful negotiations, he was able to restore a friendly atmosphere between the two groups.

The following spring, James Clark Ross used his ability to communicate with the Inuit to restock the expedition's food supply. During a sledding trip, he met another Inuit group. They invited Ross and his men to have dinner at their camp. The meal proved entertaining for both parties. The Inuit were amused by the different way Englishmen ate fish using forks and knives. Their hosts' huge appetites amazed the Englishmen. The Inuit knew their bodies needed extra supplies of fuel to help them stay warm as they worked and played in cold Arctic temperatures.

After eating, the Inuit showed Ross a pit where they kept fish frozen. Ross estimated the pit held about forty fish. He offered to trade a large knife for all of them. The Inuit accepted. Ross was surprised and a bit ashamed when he discovered the pit actually held "two hundred and twenty fish, averaging about five pounds each."[2]

The Winter of 1830–1831

When Ross returned with the salmon from the pit, the *Victory*'s crew was preparing the ship to sail. Unfortunately, the ice did not melt during that summer. The expedition was forced to spend another winter in the same spot. The second winter was monotonous. The Inuit did not return to the area. The men stayed healthy, but would have appreciated meeting with the Inuit and trading for venison and fish.[3]

Scientific research was one of the expedition's tasks. In May, James Clark Ross and a small party sledded to the North Magnetic Pole. They reached the spot on June 1 and camped near some abandoned Inuit huts. James Clark Ross made several observations with his instruments. He wanted to be sure he was as near the magnetic pole as he could possibly be. He finally marked the pole's location at 89 degrees, 59 minutes. He also noticed that the pole was moving, even while he tried to determine its location. The data he collected would help others who ventured into the Arctic later.

The explorers returned after a journey of twenty-eight days. This was the last sled journey James Clark Ross made. He drew a map of Boothia Peninsula using all the information from these treks. It remained the best map of the area for over one hundred years.

In the middle of July, the men again prepared the ship to sail, then waited for the ice to break up. Finally, on August 28, the ice drifted out of the bay and the *Victory* sailed northwest. But the ship ran aground and broke its rudder after only a few miles, making steering difficult. The next day, the crew managed to reach a harbor only fifteen miles from their winter camp. Ross named it Victory Harbour (now Victoria Harbour).

They hoped to set sail again quickly, but the broken rudder delayed their departure. Soon it was too late to venture out in the icy waterways. In Early October, Ross's expedition began to dismantle the ship for a third time. As they worked, the crew members realized that when spring came, the *Victory* would have to be abandoned. Food supplies would not last until the time it might be possible to sail north. They would have to trek northward and hope to be rescued.

Ross Abandons the *Victory*

The winter of 1831–1832 was spent making sleds and preparing gear for the summer trek. Ross decided to go overland to Fury Beach. There he could restock their food supply from Parry's cache. He also planned to use the abandoned boats to paddle east where a whaler might rescue them. In January, one crew member died.

The expedition abandoned the *Victory* on June 10. They trekked north for three weeks with three sleds piled high with provisions. Ross listed the supplies in

During the winter of 1831–1832, John Ross's crew made sleds and prepared gear for an overland trek. The expedition abandoned the Victory *on June 10.*

his report. They hauled "arms, ammunition, tools, instruments, clothing, and more."[4]

It was a difficult journey. Many of the men were sick—but all arrived safely at Fury Beach on July 2, 1832. Their first task was to build a house from old ship timbers. Canvas from the *Victory*'s sails was used for the roof. Ross called it Somerset House. Next carpenters set to work repairing the boats Parry had left behind, rigging them with sails. Gradually temperatures grew warmer and several good meals improved the men's health.

On August 1, water near the beach was free of ice. Ross's expedition set out in three boats loaded with six weeks' provisions. They hoped to reach Baffin Bay before the whalers left, but by late September, weather forced them to turn back. They reached Somerset House just before a blizzard struck. They realized no one could have survived for long if they had been caught in the snowstorm.

A Fourth Arctic Winter

During the winter of 1832–1833, one man died of scurvy. Many others grew ill. Old wounds bothered the expedition's leader, fifty-five-year-old John Ross. He feared he might not survive another winter.[5]

In the middle of August 1833, a lane of open water was spotted from the beach. Everyone worked to cut ice away from the shore. This time ice conditions allowed them to sail away in the three small boats. They made seventy-two miles toward Lancaster Sound the first day. Near the end of the month, a lookout spotted a ship's sail. The men set off after it and gradually closed on the larger ship.

Ross and his crew were taken aboard a whaler on August 26, 1833. They had been given up for dead and their rescuers were amazed when Ross identified himself. On October 18, expedition members landed in England.

Ross did not find the Northwest Passage on his second voyage. However, with the help of friendly Inuit, his crew survived four winters in the Arctic region, losing only two men. James Clark Ross also made an important contribution to science with his

---

SOURCE DOCUMENT

THE RECEPTION OF CAPTAIN ROSS IN HULL

THE HARDY VETERAN WAS DRESSED IN SEALSKIN TROUSERS WITH THE HAIR OUTWARDS OVER WHICH HE WORE A FADED NAVY UNIFORM, THE WEATHER BEATEN COUNTENANCES OF HIMSELF AND COMPANIONS BORE EVIDENCE OF THE HARDSHIPS THEY HAD UNDERGONE, ALTHOUGH THEY APPEARED TO BE IN EXCELLENT HEALTH . . . THE BELLS ARE NOW RINGING MERRILY, THE COLOURS ARE HOISTED ON NEARLY ALL THE SHIPPING IN THE PORT, AND AT 2 A PUBLIC DINNER IS TO BE GIVEN TO THE CAPTAIN BY THE PRINCIPAL INHABITANTS AT THE VICTORIA HOTEL, PREVIOUS TO HIS DEPARTURE AT 4 FOR LONDON.[6]

The London Times *printed this account of Ross's safe return to England on October 22, 1833.*

sled trip to the North Magnetic Pole. He also learned much about the Inuit culture and language.

Overland Rescue Mission

When no news of the Rosses had reached England by 1832, another expedition was sent to search for them. The commander was thirty-seven-year-old George Back. He had been a member of Franklin's land expeditions.

Back left England for Montreal, Canada, on February 17, 1833, with two other officers and eighteen men. His instructions were to go from Montreal to Great Slave Lake, then to explore a new overland route through the Canadian Arctic region, and eventually to reach Fury Beach.

During his first trek with Franklin in 1820, Back had heard of a river called the Great Fish from an old Inuit warrior. It supposedly wriggled through the tundra north and east to the Arctic Ocean. Back planned to find this river and follow it to its mouth. Then he hoped to cross over Prince Regent Inlet and search for Ross's party.

Back arrived at Fort Resolution on Great Slave Lake in August. Four days later, he set off to find the Great Fish River (now Back River). Back succeeded in finding the river, but soon had to turn around. His canoes were too weak to withstand the rapids. He spent the winter at Fort Reliance, a new base that had been built while he was gone.

While preparing for a second attempt, Back received a letter on April 30, 1834, that detailed Ross's rescue. His new orders were to explore the unknown coastline of northeastern America. With one boat and a party of twelve, he left on July 4, 1834.

After traveling twenty-five days down the Great Fish River, they sighted land across a wide waterway, Chantrey Inlet. Back continued to explore north and west along the coastline. He wanted to get as far as Point Turnagain and explore the Arctic coastline between the Great Fish and the farthest point east that Franklin had reached.

On August 16, Back headed for Fort Reliance without reaching his goal. Most likely, he feared being caught by an early Arctic winter. The river Back explored has been navigated only a few times since his expedition. His maps of the area along the Back River were used until 1948 by other explorers who dared to brave the icy Arctic regions of Canada.

The Hudson's Bay Company sent the next British expeditions in search of a Northwest Passage. It had agreed to look for a route as part of its original charter or contract with Great Britain. However, there was no profit for the company in finding the passage, so *that* part of the agreement had been ignored.

ALONG THE COAST OF NORTH AMERICA

Instead, the company had set up posts throughout the Canadian Arctic region to trade with the Inuit. Traders bartered for seal, bear, and otter pelts. Europeans wanted rare furs found only in the Arctic region. The owners wanted to continue trading with the Inuit.

Now it was time for the company's charter to be renewed. Searching for a Northwest Passage seemed to be one way to make sure the British government would renew their contract.

In 1836, the Hudson's Bay Company chose two men to lead an expedition. Peter Warren Dease already had experience exploring the Canadian Arctic. He had been a member of John Franklin's second expedition in

1825. Overland travel had changed little since then. Expeditions still explored using small boats, sleds, or on foot. Dease's experience proved useful for this trek. Thomas Simpson was chosen as the co-leader. The two were instructed to complete the job Franklin began in the 1820s. They were to fill in the blanks on the map of North America's Arctic coastline.

Dease left for Fort Chipewyan on Lake Athabasca in July 1836. Simpson stayed behind at Fort Garry (now Winnipeg) to prepare. He exercised to strengthen his body. He also studied astronomy, surveying, and mathematics. On December 1, Simpson was ready. He loaded books and instruments on a dog sled and traveled 1,277 miles to Lake Athabasca. The trip took sixty-two days. Dease was waiting there.

North for the Winter

On June 1, 1837, Dease, Simpson, and the other members of their expedition left Fort Chipewyan. They traveled north to Great Slave Lake, then down the Mackenzie River in two boats built during the winter. At a spot near Great Bear Lake, the group split in two. One party went west to build winter quarters beside the lake. Dease and Simpson continued to follow the Mackenzie with the others.

The expedition reached the Arctic Ocean on July 9. The weather was cold and foggy as they poled their boats west along the coast. They reached Return Reef two weeks later. Franklin's expedition had turned back at this point, but Dease and Simpson traveled on into uncharted territory.

By the end of July, the party had covered half the distance between Return Reef and their goal, Point Barrow. Already the short Arctic summer was drawing to an end. The weather grew colder and ice formed on the water's surface making further travel by boat impossible. Dease decided it was time to turn back, but Simpson wanted to keep going. He convinced Dease to stay and guard the boats while he went on with five men.

To Point Barrow

Simpson and five others set out on August 1 with enough pemmican and flour for twelve days. They took one canvas canoe, a kettle, and two axes. Simpson also carried instruments he used for navigation.

Trekking along the rugged shoreline was difficult. The six men frequently had to cross small streams that ran down to the sea. Progress was slow until Simpson's party met some hunters. These Inuit supplied the explorers with kayaks, skin boats that floated easily in shallow water. This made it possible for the small group to make better time as they paddled west, hugging the shoreline.

On August 4, Simpson spotted "the long spit of gravel hummocks that was Point Barrow."[1] He and his men forced their way through the ice forming on the water near shore, then paddled more than half a mile across a bay. When they arrived at Point Barrow, the explorers cheered and raised the British flag. There was little time to celebrate though. The next morning they had to head back to the place where Dease was waiting. Then the expedition retraced their route along the coastline and up the Mackenzie River. The entire party arrived safely at Fort Confidence, their winter quarters, in late September.

During the long Arctic winter, Dease and Simpson began planning for another expedition. This time they would explore the coastline east of the area Franklin had surveyed. Simpson scouted a route from Great Bear Lake to the Coppermine River. He and two men traveled more than one hundred miles overland. They made the trip twice during the winter even though temperatures sometimes dropped to minus 60 degrees. On the second trip, Simpson and his men carried provisions and stored them near the Coppermine River. This would be the starting point for Dease and Simpson's next mission.

Two More Ventures

Dease and Simpson's second expedition left Fort Confidence on June 6, 1838. They marched overland to the Coppermine River and prepared to launch their boats. Water flowed dangerously high between the river's banks. They started downstream anyway, trying to avoid loose chunks of ice carried along by the swift current. The boats reached the mouth of the river safely about the middle of July. Now the expedition headed east along the shores of the Arctic Ocean, hopefully to complete the work Franklin had begun. Progress was slow and difficult, for little ice had melted that summer. Chunks frequently smashed against the boats, damaging the sides. The explorers decided that a layer of protective copper over the bow would have prevented some of the damage.

On August 6, Simpson climbed to the top of a high cliff. From there, he saw Coronation Gulf. It was still covered with ice. He remembered that Franklin had found open water in the gulf on the same date.

Two weeks later, Dease decided it was time to start back, even though they had not reached Point Turnagain where Franklin had turned around. Once again, Simpson talked Dease into waiting with the boats while he and a party of men went on. Simpson hoped to reach Point Turnagain and cover a little more ground than Franklin had. He agreed to rejoin Dease by the end of August.

Thomas Simpson and his men set out on foot, traveling along the uneven shoreline. The men were loaded down with heavy packs. Their feet were often wet and cold from fording through icy streams. Conditions were miserable, but Simpson and his party trekked east for five more days. They passed Point Turnagain and surveyed more than one hundred miles of unexplored coastline before going back to join Peter Warren Dease. The entire party arrived safely at Fort Confidence on October 14, 1838.

The Missing Pieces

Dease and Simpson made one more expedition during the summer of 1839. This journey was more successful. The weather was better, and the explorers got an early start down the Coppermine River.

When they reached Coronation Gulf, Simpson discovered it was nearly free of ice. The gulf had been frozen over the year before. They sailed easily across and spotted an open waterway at the east end. This strait flowed between the North American continent and Victoria Island. The group navigated the strait, later named for Dease, and then traveled across Queen Maud Gulf.

At the end of the gulf, the expedition spotted another waterway (now called Simpson Strait). It too was free of ice. They sailed through and soon realized that this strait led to Chantry Inlet. Across the inlet was the mouth of Back's Great Fish River, territory that had already been charted.

Now, Simpson and Dease knew they had nearly completed the job they had set out to do. Three days later, the explorers reached an island near the river's mouth. There they found provisions of pemmican, chocolate, and gunpowder. George Back had cached these supplies during his exploration along the river named for him.

Simpson explored another forty miles eastward to the mouths of the Castor and Pollux rivers. He also trekked along the south shores of both King William and Victoria islands. Then the expedition headed back

SOURCE DOCUMENT

"I AND I *ALONE* HAVE THE WELL-EARNED HONOUR . . . OF
UNFURLING THE BRITISH FLAG ON POINT BARROW. FAME I
WILL HAVE, BUT IT MUST BE ALONE."[2]

*Dease and Simpson are both recognized for their
exploration of the Canadian Arctic coast. However, in
private letters, Simpson claimed that he alone deserved
the fame. He wanted to be the sole commander of the
next expedition he planned.*

to Great Bear Lake. They arrived at Fort Confidence
on September 24, 1839. The Hudson's Bay expedition
had covered 1,631 miles during that summer. This was
the longest voyage ever made in boats on the Arctic
Ocean.

Dease and Simpson completed the work Franklin
had begun in the 1820s. They traveled west from
Return Reef to Point Barrow and east beyond Point
Turnagain. They charted whole new stretches of the
coast of North America. They explored by boat, on
foot, and by kayak; but they did not discover the
Northwest Passage.

Simpson was convinced that he would find the passage on his next expedition. Unfortunately, he died
before Hudson's Bay Company approved his plan. The
trading company decided not to fund any more Arctic
explorations.

SEARCH AND DISCOVERY

More explorers went north to brave the icy waters of the Canadian Arctic by the mid-1800s. These men sailed in search of the Northwest Passage. They also hoped to find signs of Sir John Franklin's expedition. Franklin had sailed with two ships and a crew of 128 men on May 19, 1845. No one had seen or heard from the expedition since the end of August that year.

In 1847, Sir John Ross, an experienced Arctic explorer, suggested that another ship be sent to search for Franklin. The Royal Navy agreed to send a party overland to leave stores of food. No rescue ships were sent until a year later.

More expeditions went north looking for survivors of Franklin's party in 1850. The British Royal Navy sent two. Lady Jane Franklin, Sir John's wife, used her own money and donations from friends to equip one of the rescue ships.

In August, several expeditions met near the northwest end of Lancaster Sound. They were planning where to search next, when the first clues of Franklin and his men were discovered. Three graves were found on Beechey Island. Dates on the graves showed that Franklin had spent his second winter here in 1846. Now the expeditions decided to search further north.

One British expedition led by William Penny sent out a number of sled parties during the spring of 1851 looking for Franklin. They did not turn back until food supplies grew low. Penny believed search parties should continue to look in the area of Wellington Channel. (This later proved to be the direction Franklin went.) Unfortunately, he failed to convince the others that Wellington should be searched, and the expeditions returned to England.

From the Pacific

Another British team also was sent out in 1850 to search for Franklin. They were to enter the Arctic region from the Pacific Ocean. Two ships, the *Enterprise*, under the command of Captain Richard Collinson, and the *Investigator*, led by Commander Robert McClure, left England together in January. They crossed the Atlantic and sailed around the tip of South America. Then the two ships lost sight of each other in the stormy South Pacific. They sailed north along the coasts of South America, then North America, hoping to find each other.

McClure reached the Arctic Ocean near the end of the summer. Using his ship as a battering ram, he sailed into the ice-filled waters. Collinson arrived in the far north too late to follow the *Investigator*. He spent the winter in a safe port and then tried to catch

McClure the next summer. Collinson and his crew sailed up the Prince of Wales Strait and discovered the place where McClure had spent the previous winter. From there, the *Enterprise* tried to sail north along the coast of Banks Island, the direction they believed McClure had gone. Unfortunately, thick ice had already formed in the strait, and the ship could not break through. The *Enterprise* was forced south. There they found safe winter quarters in Walker Bay on Victoria Island.

During the spring, Collinson sent sled parties to search nearby areas for Franklin and McClure. They found no sign of either expedition. When Collinson's ship broke free of the ice in early August 1852, he explored Prince Albert Sound on the west coast of Victoria Island. Then the *Enterprise* went south and east around the Wollaston Peninsula, through Dolphin and Union straits, Coronation Gulf, and Dease Strait. This was an amazing feat of navigation. The *Enterprise* was a sailing ship that weighed over four hundred tons. The large ship could sometimes bash through ice-filled water. However, if there was not enough wind to move it along, crew members rowing small boats towed it through the water. This was hard, tiring work, even in good conditions.

The *Enterprise* spent one more winter in the Arctic region in Cambridge Bay, near the east end of Dease Strait. Again, Collinson sent sled parties to search for Franklin, but they found no trace of the lost expedition. After 1,164 days in the Arctic Ocean, Collinson sailed for home in August 1854. The *Enterprise* rounded Point Barrow and escaped the ice pack. They arrived in England in May of 1855.

The Missing Link

McClure and the *Investigator* had made their way around Point Barrow in the summer of 1850 and sailed east along the shores that Franklin, Dease, and Simpson had charted. They worked their way slowly past the mouth of the Mackenzie River. On the Canadian coast, they met a group of Inuit who had never seen white men before. The huge ships amazed the Inuit. They thought the vessels had been carved from one enormous tree and wanted to know where these trees grew.

McClure and his officers were not favorably impressed with the Inuit they met. One officer recorded that these people were: "the most filthy race on the face of the globe . . . thieving, cunning . . . treacherous and deceitful (dishonest)."[1]

The *Investigator* continued east. McClure discovered Prince of Wales Strait between Banks and Victoria islands. As the ship sailed up the strait, the ice grew thicker. By October, they could go no farther. McClure ordered his crew to prepare the ship for winter.

That same month, McClure set out with a sled party to explore the area and search for Franklin. They worked their way up the eastern shore of Banks Island to the northern end of Prince of Wales Strait. From there, they looked across the ice-choked sound to

On April 7, 1853, Robert McClure and seven of his men, along with the rescue party completed the final connection of the Northwest Passage.

Melville Island some sixty miles away. McClure studied maps of the waterways east of Melville Sound. He now felt certain that a water passage between the Atlantic and the Pacific oceans existed. In fact, the captain and his crew were looking out across the missing link in the Northwest Passage.

McClure had a close call on his way back to the *Investigator*. He had rushed on ahead of his crew and lost the trail. The captain spent one freezing Arctic night trying to find the ship. When he finally got back, McClure was too exhausted to speak. His legs and arms were stiff from the cold. He looked more dead than alive.

When McClure recovered from this misadventure, he made a formal announcement to his crew. He felt certain that they had discovered the final link to the Northwest Passage. Everyone would share the reward offered by Parliament.

In the spring, sled crews were sent out to search for Franklin. They explored up and down the Prince of Wales Strait and along the coasts of Victoria and Banks islands. Unfortunately, no trace of the lost expedition was found.

One sled party did find something interesting—a new band of Inuit. McClure decided to visit these people. He hoped they might tell him something about Franklin's lost expedition or provide information that would help him map the area.

The captain was surprised when one Inuit woman drew an almost perfect chart of the area on the paper he gave her.[2] Her map filled in the blanks along the coastline of North America. It also showed that Wollaston Island was actually a peninsula on the southwest coast of Victoria Island. Unfortunately, the Inuit had no information to share about Franklin and his men.

The Northwest Passage

The following summer McClure tried to sail east through the Melville sound and complete the Northwest Passage, but ice blocked the route. The expedition was again forced to winter near Banks Island.

In fact, the *Investigator* remained trapped in the ice for the next two winters. By March 1853, their food supply had to be rationed. Many men were ill with scurvy. McClure decided his crew had to abandon ship. He wrote a detailed report of their explorations and how they had found the Northwest Passage. Then he announced his plan to the crew. Twenty of the strongest men would stay with the ship. The others would try to reach civilization by two different routes. One party would follow the Mackenzie River overland. The second group would man a small boat and set sail for the whaling area in Baffin Bay.

On April 5, as the crew prepared to set off, one of the men selected to leave died of scurvy. This delayed the departure. The following day, a sailor rushed up to announce "that something black was moving on the ice to the east, a muskox perhaps." But it was not an animal. "They are men," another sailor cried, "First a man, then a sledge with men."[3]

The Investigator *was trapped in the ice for two winters before McClure decided to abandon ship.*

Help had arrived. Members of another British expedition had found McClure's ship. The rescuers were shocked by the crew's physical condition.[4] They were even more surprised to learn that the starving sailors' next meal consisted of only a tiny piece of bread and a cup of weak cocoa. The rescuers pulled bacon from the loaded sled and prepared a hearty meal.

On April 7, 1853, McClure, seven of his men, and the rescue party trekked back across the strait. This crossing completed the final connection of the Northwest Passage. When McClure and his crew returned to England, Parliament awarded them the prize of ten thousand pounds for this discovery.

SOURCE DOCUMENT

THE ANNOUNCEMENT OF RELIEF BEING CLOSE AT HAND, WHEN NONE WAS SUPPOSED TO BE EVEN WITHIN THE ARCTIC CIRCLE, WAS TOO SUDDEN, UNEXPECTED, AND JOYOUS FOR OUR MINDS TO COMPREHEND IT AT ONCE. THE NEWS FLEW WITH LIGHTENING RAPIDITY, THE SHIP WAS ALL IN COMMOTION; THE SICK FORGOT THEIR MALADIES, LEAPT FROM THEIR HAMMOCKS . . . THEY ALL RUSHED FOR THE HATCHWAY TO BE ASSURED THAT A STRANGER WAS ACTUALLY AMONGST THEM AND THAT HIS TALE WAS TRUE.[5]

McClure recorded his crew's surprised and happy reaction upon being rescued in The Discovery of the North-West Passage, *his report of* Investigator's *four years in the Arctic region.*

However, McClure eventually lost his claim to the Northwest Passage. It was later discovered that some of Franklin's men had probably found another passage two years earlier. They walked from Victoria Strait, near King William Island, to Simpson Strait. This strait connected the area Franklin had explored during his land expeditions.[6] Public opinion favored Sir John Franklin and his crew. They had lost their lives in the Arctic region as they searched for the elusive Northwest Passage.

By the end of the search for Franklin, several Northwest Passages had been discovered. One route went through Prince of Wales Strait. A second followed Bellot and Rae straits. Peel Sound to Rae Strait and M'Clure Strait to Viscount Melville Sound were also routes. None of these proved to be reliable passages. Fifty

NAVIGATING THE PASSAGE

years went by before anyone sailed through any Arctic waterway from the Atlantic to the Pacific. Roald Amundsen made the first successful passage in 1906.

Roald grew up in Norway. During his childhood, he read everything he could find about Franklin and the search for the Northwest Passage. He wanted to be an Arctic explorer when he grew up. Roald played football, skied, and climbed mountains to build strong muscles. He even left his bedroom window open during the long winter nights to get used to freezing temperatures.

In 1893, Amundsen wanted to sign on as a member of a Norwegian expedition to the North Pole. His mother refused to let him go. She wanted him to be a doctor, not an explorer. Later that year, Amundsen's mother died. Now, the twenty-one year old was free to follow his dream.

Learning From the Past

Amundsen studied reports of other Arctic explorers. He tried to identify problems so he could avoid making the same mistakes. The young explorer discovered that many expedition leaders had no navigation skills. They had to depend on the advice of the ship's captain as they sailed the icy waterways. He also realized that the scientific staff and sailors often did not work well together.

To solve these problems, Amundsen studied navigation and science, and mastered both. He planned to take only a few carefully selected crew members. Everyone would help sail the boat and carry out scientific research.

In 1900, he bought a little wooden fishing boat, the *Gjøa*. It was equipped with sails and a small engine. Compared to ships used on other expeditions, this boat was a minnow. After studying the Arctic waterways, Amundsen believed his little ship could make its way through. "What has not been accomplished by large vessels and main force," he said, "I will attempt with a small vessel and patience."[1]

For the next two years, Amundsen continued to prepare. He took the *Gjøa* on a training cruise and got his master's certificate in navigation. He learned how to care for and handle dogs and sleds and interviewed crew members and other Arctic explorers. Finally, he was ready to set sail.

The Voyage Begins

On June 16, 1903, Amundsen, age twenty-nine, departed from Oslo, Norway, with a crew of six and several dogs. The *Gjøa* was loaded with equipment and provisions needed to spend five years in the Arctic. The explorer planned to navigate the Northwest Passage and locate the North Magnetic Pole. On August 22, Amundsen landed at Beechey Island, one of Franklin's winter camps. From there, the *Gjøa* sailed south through Peel Sound and into Franklin Strait.

The voyage went smoothly until the end of August. Then, the *Gjøa*'s engine room caught fire. Twenty-two hundred gallons of kerosene was stored in nearby compartments. It seemed certain the kerosene would explode, but the crew did not panic. They worked together and put the fire out before it reached the kerosene.

The very next day, the expedition ran into more trouble. The ship ran aground on a reef. To lighten their load, Amundsen and his men threw ten thousand pounds of food for the sled dogs over board, but the *Gjøa* stuck tight. Then high winds flung the boat against a rock, splintering her keel. Fearing the ship might break apart, Amundsen ordered the lifeboats loaded with emergency supplies. As the crew prepared to abandon ship, the wind suddenly picked the *Gjøa* up. The bottom of the boat thumped over the rocky

Roald Amundsen was the first to sail through the Northwest Passage in 1906.

reef, then finally slid into deep water. Everyone was amazed and relieved to find they were still afloat.[2]

Under sail again, the crew moved down the east coast of King William Island through James Ross Strait and into Rae Strait. Amundsen anchored in a little harbor on the southeast corner of King William Island. This would be their home for the next two years. Amundsen named it Gjøa Haven.

Learning New Lessons

Every crew member was quickly assigned a task. Some set off to hunt caribou, stockpiling meat for the winter. Others built observatories for magnetic and astrological observations, a supply hut, and another small shelter for two of the crew to live in. The rest bunked on the *Gjøa*. Their winter camp was nearly finished when a band of friendly Netsilik arrived. Though their ancestors had met up with British explorers many years before, these Inuit had never seen a white man.

Amundsen immediately made friends with the Netsilik. They taught the explorer and his crew skills important for survival in the harsh Arctic climate. The explorer later used this knowledge in the Antarctic region. One man showed them how to build snow houses using a long-handled knife. The Netsiliks laughed at the explorers' first attempts, but the Norwegians did not give up.[3] They knew that snow houses were warmer than tents.

The Inuit taught the white men to fight frostbite by removing a warm hand from a glove and rubbing the cold spot vigorously. They showed them how to dress for below-freezing temperatures. The Netsiliks' parkas and trousers were loose, fast-drying, and windproof. Undergarments were made of deerskin that was warm to the touch when put on. They wore special gloves with long cuffs. The cuffs were tied tightly around the arm to keep snow out. The group also showed Amundsen their deerskin stockings with fur on the inside and deer skin footgear stuffed with grass that absorbed moisture and dried out quickly at night. Three weeks after making camp, Amundsen had his own set of deerskin clothing. For the next twenty months, he and his crew dressed like the Inuit.

In addition to teaching the explorers how to dress, the Netsilik taught them to paddle kayaks and to coat sled runners with a film of ice. This allowed the sleds to slide more smoothly across snow and ice.

Another important lesson the explorers learned was the value of patience. The Inuit always traveled at a slow but steady pace as they moved from place to place. Getting sweaty and then chilled was dangerous in frigid Arctic temperatures. Netsiliks arrived at their destinations more slowly, but stayed healthy because they knew how to stay dry and warm.

North Magnetic Pole

The winter was spent preparing for a sled trip to the North Magnetic Pole. The crew practiced driving the dogs in the frigid Arctic conditions. On March 1, 1904, Amundsen and three others set out, but soon discovered that temperatures were still too cold. He also learned that his dogs could only pull enough supplies and equipment for two people. All future sled trips were limited to two men.

In April, the weather improved. Amundsen and one crew member set off again toward the North Magnetic Pole. At first, the dogs did not pull properly. Amundsen soon realized that the team disliked running into a completely white landscape. He tried skiing ahead of them. The dogs raced after him, pulling the sled quickly over the snow.

Amundsen reached the spot where James Clark Ross had located the pole. There he discovered that magnetic north had moved some thirty miles. His information that the pole was not fixed was important scientific data. During this trek, the young explorer also realized that the unnavigated section of the Northwest Passage was only about one hundred fifty miles.

The following spring, Amundsen completed his scientific studies. In June 1905, the crew began packing up.

The Missing Link

On August 12, 1905, Amundsen and his crew set sail from Gjøa Haven. Fog hampered their progress through the strait named for Thomas Simpson. The crew followed the Netsilik in kayaks through the waters where no white man had sailed before.

"We bungled through zigzag as if we were drunk," Amundsen said.[4] The lookout in the crow's nest pointed first one way then the other to avoid rocks and small islands in the channel. After five days of difficult sailing, the *Gjøa* edged through ice floes into Victoria Strait and anchored in Cambridge Bay. August 17, 1905, was a date worth remembering. Amundsen and his crew had sailed their ship through the last watery link of the Northwest Passage. They were back in charted territory. Collinson and the *Enterprise* had wintered in this bay.

Sailing was much easier for the next several days. Amundsen used Collinson's descriptions to navigate Dease Strait, Coronation Gulf, and Dolphin and Union straits. On August 26, the *Gjøa* neared Banks Island and entered a large bay later named Amundsen Gulf. That same morning the crew sighted a ship. Amundsen knew it had come from the Pacific Ocean.

SOURCE DOCUMENT

THE NORTH WEST PASSAGE HAD BEEN ACCOMPLISHED—MY DREAM FROM CHILDHOOD. THIS VERY MOMENT IT WAS FULFILLED. I HAD A PECULIAR SENSATION IN MY THROAT; I WAS SOMEWHAT OVERWORKED AND TIRED, AND I SUPPOSE IT WAS WEAKNESS ON MY PART, BUT I COULD FEEL TEARS COMING TO MY EYES. "VESSEL IN SIGHT!" THE WORDS WERE MAGICAL.[5]

This statement sums up Amundsen's pleasure when he realized he had completed the first successful voyage through the Northwest Passage.

When the schooner pulled alongside, Captain James McKenna shook Amundsen's hand. Then the captain said, "I am exceedingly pleased to be the first one to welcome you on getting through the North West Passage."[6]

Another Arctic Winter

A few weeks later, heavy pack ice stopped the *Gjøa* near the mouth of the Mackenzie River in northern Canada. Amundsen's crew prepared to spend the winter at King Point. However, Amundsen was eager to report his accomplishment to the world. He decided to travel overland to the nearest telegraph post. The closest post was five hundred miles south on the other side of a nine-thousand foot mountain range in Eagle City, Alaska.

The young explorer arrived in Eagle on December 5, 1905. From the U.S. Army telegraph station, Amundsen sent a one-thousand-word message announcing his successful voyage through the Northwest Passage to the world. By this time, he was out of money. The fee to send such a long telegram was more than seven hundred dollars. The explorer sent his announcement collect to a friend in Norway.

After traveling one thousand miles by ski and dog sled, Amundsen returned to his ship and crew in March. The days lengthened and summer arrived in the Arctic region. By early July, the crew was ready to sail west again. Near Point Barrow fog, high winds, drifting ice, and shallow water made navigation difficult.

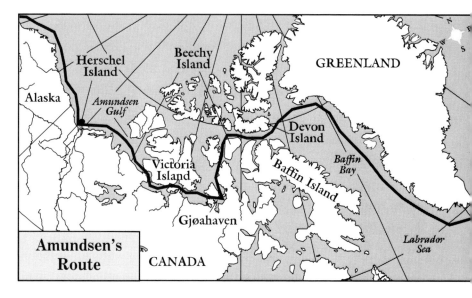

After their ship was stuck in the ice over the winter, Amundsen and his crew at last completed the first navigation through the Northwest Passage.

Finally, on August 30, 1906, Amundsen and his little fishing boat passed through the Bering Strait. The Norwegians had completed the first navigation of the Northwest Passage. A huge crowd welcomed the *Gjøa* when the expedition reached Nome, Alaska.

At Long Last

The successful completion of his voyage through the Northwest Passage fulfilled Amundsen's childhood dream. His journey proved the passage was not a practical route for large ships carrying goods between Asia and Europe. Only small boats like the *Gjøa* could hope to complete the passage through Simpson Strait. It was thirty-four years before another little ship, the *St. Roch*, would make this passage again.

For more than three centuries, since Martin Frobisher's day, the Northwest Passage had defeated the world's best seamen. Roald Amundsen finally captured the prize through careful planning, and great common sense. His most important tool, though, proved to be the example of the Netsilik—people who knew their Arctic home the best. By adapting traditional Inuit ways, Amundsen conquered the Northwest Passage.

10

THE NORTHWEST PASSAGE ON THE MAP

Over five hundred years have passed since early explorers sailed off to try to discover a Northwest Passage. These courageous men explored the seas to the west and north. They hoped to find a shorter, more reliable trade route from Europe to China. They sought their fortune, hoping to bring home shiploads of silk, gold, ivory, and unusual animals and plants from the east.

The voyages of Henry Cabot, Giovanni da Verrazzano, and Martin Frobisher proved there was no easy water route west. They discovered a huge landmass, the continent of North America, blocked the way. Early explorers mapped large areas of this new territory during their voyages. They also discovered new fishing areas, groups of people, and lands that could be colonized.

The need for a trade route between Europe and China grew less important as time passed. Still explorers continued to go north. Captains, like Henry Hudson and James Cook, risked their lives for adventure. They made exploring undiscovered lands and waters a career. Their discoveries in North America opened a new continent for settlers who followed the explorers west and built colonies.

Over the years, many men and ships were lost while sailing or trekking into unknown icy regions. When explorers set out, they knew they might not return home. Still they searched for a Northwest Passage.

During the twentieth century, a new Arctic route was explored. In August 1960, United States Commander George Steele sailed in the *Seadragon*. His ship was a modern nuclear-powered submarine. Steel's assignment was to find an underwater route through the Arctic region. The commander and his crew discovered a passage under the ice. They traveled through Baffin Bay and Parry Channel to the Arctic Ocean. At the geographic North Pole, the sub surfaced. The crew climbed out on the ice to play softball before continuing through the Bering Strait to Pearl Harbor in Hawaii.

After oil was discovered in Alaska, the passage was once more considered as a shipping route. The first oil tanker, the supertanker *Manhattan*, successfully traveled the length of the icy passage in 1969. These tankers were specially equipped ships known as icebreakers. Even with this modern technology, cruising through the Arctic waterways was not easy.

What makes these expeditions important even today? Why should one study the records of expeditions that went north and west? What can be learned from the legacy Arctic exploration left behind?

The Map of the World

A globe of the world shows significant discoveries made by Arctic explorers. The map is labeled with straits and bays named after those who first sailed or trekked through that region. Explorers are remembered by points and waterways bearing their name. Names became navigational aids. They helped ships locate their position as they sailed through the many Arctic passageways. These names also helped establish territorial claims.

Each expedition left its own mark. Explorers recorded details about new territories on the charts. This new information helped future explorers. As they retraced these routes, they tried to go a little bit farther each time into new regions.

History can be tracked from south to north starting with Cabot Strait and Hudson and Frobisher bays. Waterways farther north have been named for those men who studied the discoveries of earlier explorers, then sailed on into unknown regions. The names of Davis Strait and Baffin Bay record for all time the places these men discovered.

From the northern edge of Baffin Bay, the search for the Northwest Passage turned west. Now the historical route becomes more difficult to track. The explorers who ventured deeper into the Canadian Arctic region zigzagged their way through the maze of icy waterways. In the very heart of the Arctic region, straits are named for Franklin, James Ross, Dease, and Simpson. Even further west, near the Beaufort Sea, another familiar name appears. Amundsen Gulf marks the final link and the end of the long, eventful search for the Northwest Passage.

Trade and Commerce

Explorers who searched for a passage did not find a reliable trade route to China. The newly discovered territory offered opportunities of its own. Trading companies, like the Hudson's Bay Company, quickly took advantage of these new resources. Posts were set up throughout the Canadian Arctic region to trade with the Inuit. Traders bartered for seal, bear, and otter pelts. Europeans wanted rare furs found only in the Arctic. Inuit also found the trading companies beneficial. They wanted goods—guns, ammunition, clothing, tea, and tobacco—that the white men imported. It meant they did not have to depend entirely upon fishing and hunting for survival.

The Canadian fur industry was profitable. Later, other valuable resources were found hidden in the frigid Arctic region: gold, silver, and underground pools of oil. These discoveries drew more and more settlers into the northern regions. Many only came for what they could take away. Others settled down and built communities that still exist today.

Scientific Research

Many went north simply for the purpose of exploring new territory. Scientific research was often one of the tasks assigned to these expeditions. The equipment used by early explorers was simple. A sailor who showed a talent for sketching would draw what he observed. Others might collect fish from the sea and plants from the places where they went ashore. Daily logs and journals were used to record weather and ice conditions. Temperatures and other natural occurrences that happened during the voyage were noted. This basic information helped others who ventured into the Arctic later.

More expeditions traveled north. They continued to collect scientific data. New species of plant and animal life were discovered. Records were made about new civilizations. These scientists learned firsthand how frigid temperatures affect men, animals, tools, and materials. The movement of the pack ice aided understanding of currents in the Arctic Ocean. All this information added to the store of general knowledge about life in Arctic regions.

New information is still being discovered about how the area is changing. Researchers have noted a warming trend in the Arctic region. It is causing the ice caps to shrink. If this continues, the Northwest Passage may become a dependable shortcut. Today, ships traveling from Europe to China must go south through the Panama or Suez canals. A polar shipping route north of Canada would be shorter by more than four thousand miles.

The warming trend does pose an environmental threat to the area. Less ice pack and more ship traffic could change the feeding habits of fish, seal, and polar bears. This could threaten the Inuit way of life. They still depend on Arctic animals for survival.

The quest for scientific information continues to draw scientists to the Arctic. Research teams work in this frigid area, hoping to add to our understanding of its unique environment.

New Peoples

From the very beginning, explorers saw signs that people inhabited even the coldest Arctic regions. This was a great opportunity to learn about new cultures and how the Inuit survived in extreme conditions.

The Inuit helped the Arctic explorers adapt to extreme conditions. This modern-day Inuit holds a fishing net.

For the most part, though, early explorers made little effort to get to know Arctic inhabitants. Racial prejudice made them unwilling to listen or learn from the Inuit. This was unfortunate. Because of this, ships were crushed by ice, tons of equipment lost, and many men buried in the Arctic region.

Amundsen, who made the first successful voyage through the Northwest Passage, adopted Inuit ways. He dressed in clothing made of fur and skins. He learned to drive dogsleds and to build igloos from blocks of snow. He hunted with the Inuit and ate the same food. This knowledge helped him stay healthy and survive for more than eighteen months in the Arctic region. He used these methods again to beat British naval officer Robert F. Scott to the South Pole on the continent of Antarctica.

Today, the different groups that make their home in Arctic regions have been studied. People who live in warmer climates have gained a new respect for the ways of these peoples. Information has been recorded about how they dress, build houses and boats, hunt, and prepare and preserve food. Records have been made of Inuit legends, games, and beliefs. Museums have been built to share their history. These resources help us understand and know the people of the north. In addition, this information has made it easier for those who set out to explore the Arctic region to survive to tell their tale.

It is important to preserve the unique heritage of Arctic groups. As in all parts of the world, change has

DURING THE VOYAGE OF THE GJØA WE CAME INTO CONTACT WITH TEN DIFFERENT ESKIMO TRIBES IN ALL, AND WE HAD GOOD OPPORTUNITIES OF OBSERVING THE INFLUENCE OF CIVILIZATION ON THEM, AS WE WERE ABLE TO COMPARE THOSE ESKIMO WHO HAD COME INTO CONTACT WITH CIVILIZATION WITH THOSE WHO HAD NOT. AND I MUST STATE IT AS MY FIRM CONVICTION THAT THE LATTER, THE ESKIMO LIVING ABSOLUTELY ISOLATED FROM CIVILIZATION OF ANY KIND, ARE UNDOUBTEDLY THE HAPPIEST, HEALTHIEST, AND MOST HONOURABLE AND MORE CONTENTED AMONG THEM . . . MY SINCEREST WISH FOR OUR FRIENDS THE NETSILIK ESKIMOS IS, THAT CIVILIZATION MAY *NEVER* REACH THEM.[1]

Amundsen did not believe that the Inuit benefited from contact with white men. He found that groups with little contact with outsiders were happier, healthier, and more content with their way of life.

come to the Arctic region. The influence of technology and contact with other cultures has permanently changed the way of life of these groups.

Discover the Northwest Passage Today

Most travelers will not venture north by ship or foot to explore the Arctic firsthand. Instead, books and videos will be their best resources to learn about the Northwest Passage. Words and images will move them along the icy waters of the Arctic region and through the snow-packed landscapes. In this way, anyone can study the geography, the plants and animals, and the peoples of the region.

For those who are brave of heart, there is another way to explore the icy area. If you choose to travel north, plan to stop at the Northwest Passage Territorial Historical Park. It is located in and around the village of Gjøa Haven on King William Island.

In the park, visitors are invited to follow a self-guided trail. They can read tales about failed expeditions and the story of Roald Amundsen's successful voyage. The trail begins in the park's museum. Here visitors find displays that feature a replica of Amundsen's ship, the *Gjøa*, and photos taken by one of his crew during their stay. More exhibits tell the stories of Sir John Franklin and other explorers who searched for the Northwest Passage. Visitors also learn about the Netsilik people who inhabit the area. Traditional tools used by the Inuit such as uluit, or

In 1900, Amundsen bought a little wooden fishing boat, the Gjøa. After studying the Arctic waterways, Amundsen believed his little ship could make its way through.

women's knives, and kakivait, hunters' spears, are on display. Caribou clothing, water containers, and kayaks can also be studied.

Outside the museum, the first stop along the trail is the "magnet," a shelter Amundsen used in his observation of the North Magnetic Pole. The explorer and his men built the shelter from packing crates filled with sand and covered with sailcloth. They were careful not to use copper nails in the crates. Those nails would have interfered with magnetic readings.

The next site along the trail is the observatory Amundsen built to house his scientific instruments. Nearby, a third spot shows where fresh drinking water was collected from a lake.

The fourth site describes Gjøa Haven. Amundsen called it "the finest little harbor in the world."[2] From this vantage point, visitors can study the natural features of the harbor. The deep, narrow inlet provides a safe haven from massive pack ice and stormy seas.

The remains of Franklin's crew, discovered on the southwest corner of King William Island, are buried at the next stop. It serves as a sad reminder of the challenges facing Arctic expeditions. This is one of many gravesites scattered across the North.

The walk ends at the Hudson's Bay Company building. A supply ship is docked nearby. Vessels like this delivered supplies such as guns and ammunition, food, clothing, tea, and tobacco to the Hudson's Bay posts across the North. Having these trade goods available changed forever the lifestyle of the Netsilik people who lived in the area.

The Solution to a Riddle

Now, the riddle that Sir John Franklin, Captain Cook, and many others sailed off to search for has been solved. We know that a waterway between Europe and Asia does exist. The Northwest Passage runs south of Iceland and Greenland. From there, ships must travel north and west through the Islands of the Canadian Arctic region, then along the northern coast of Alaska. We also know, that in spite of all the data collected over the last five hundred years, navigating the passage from one end to the other remains a challenge—even for modern explorers.

★ TIMELINE ★

1497—John Cabot sails in the *Mathew* and discovers Newfoundland.

1524—Giovanni da Verrazzano explores the coast of North America from the Carolinas to Newfoundland.

1534 -1536—Jacques Cartier searches for the Northwest Passage and discovers the Gulf of St. Lawrence and the St. Lawrence River.

1576—Martin Frobisher explores Frobisher Bay and Baffin Island.

1585—John Davis maps Davis Strait and returns to England convinced that a Northwest Passage did exist.

1610 -1611—Henry Hudson set off on his fourth and final voyage; he discovers Hudson Strait and Bay; Hudson is set adrift in Hudson Bay by mutineers.

1616—Robert Bylot and William Baffin explore Baffin Bay and discover and name Lancaster, Jones, and Smith sounds.

1776 -1779—Captain James Cook tries to find a Northwest Passage from the Pacific entrance to the Arctic Ocean; He is killed by Hawaiians on the Hawaiian Islands.

1818—John Ross sails up Lancaster Sound some thirty miles then spotted what he believed to be mountains blocking their route.

1819 —John Franklin sets off from York Factory in
−1821   Canada on his first overland Arctic Expedition;
Only five men survive this trek.

1819 —William Parry explores Lancaster Sound,
−1823   sailing through the "mountains" Ross had
spotted. He discovers Melville Island.

1825 —John Franklin completes a second, more
−1827   successful expedition along the Canadian
Arctic coast.

1828 —John Ross and James Clark Ross spend four
−1833   winters in the Arctic region; James Clark Ross
sleds to the North Magnetic Pole; The
expedition abandons their ship in 1832; A
whaler rescues surviving members of the
expedition on August 26, 1833.

1833 —George Back is sent to search for the Ross
−1834   expedition; After Ross returns safely to
England, Back explores the Canadian River
that now bears his name.

1836 —Peter Warren Dease and Thomas Simpson lead
−1839   two expeditions along the Canadian Arctic
coast; They complete the job that Franklin
had started.

1845 —Sir John Franklin expedition sails in search of
the Northwest Passage; Last report of his
party arrives in England that same August.

1850—Several expeditions searching for Franklin meet near Beechey Island and discover graves; the site proves to be Franklin's winter camp in 1846; Two ships under the commands of Robert McClure and Richard Collinson are sent to search for Franklin from the Pacific side; They become separated in the Pacific; McClure enters the Arctic Ocean and prepares to winter near Banks Island; On an overland sled trip McClure sights the final link to the Northwest Passage.

1851 –1855—Collinson sails after McClure unsuccessfully; He and his crew spend 1,164 days in the Arctic Ocean searching for Franklin; they arrive in England in May 1855. McClure and his crew spend two winters trapped in the ice; they are rescued on April 6, 1853, by another British expedition that had entered the Arctic region from the east. The first Northwest Passage was completed by ship and on foot on April 7, 1853.

1903 –1906—Roald Amundsen completes the first successful sea transit of the Northwest Passage.

1960—In August, Commander George Steele navigates an underwater Northwest Passage in the nuclear-powered submarine *Seadragon*.

1969—The oil tanker *Manhattan* travels the length of the Northwest Passage for the first time; Its crew fixes approximate location of North Magnetic Pole.

★ Chapter Notes ★

Chapter 1. Franklin's Final Voyage

1. Ann Sutton and Myron Sutton, *Journey Into Ice: John Franklin and the Northwest Passage* (New York: Rand McNally & Company, 1965), p. 217.

2. Scott Cookman, *Ice Blink: the Tragic Fate of Sir John Franklin's Lost Polar Expedition* (New York: John Wiley & Sons, Inc., 2000), p. 209.

3. Sutton and Sutton, p. 219.

4. Ann Savours, *The Search for the North West Passage* (New York: St. Martin's Press, 1999), p. 199.

5. "Lord Franklin," *Songs and Ballads about Sir John Franklin*, n.d., <www.ric.edu/rpotter/lord.html> (December 11, 2003).

6. Savours, p. 273.

7. *Sir John Franklin*, <www.britannica.com/eb/article?idxref=29347> (May 5, 2001).

8. Cookman, p. 203.

9. Ibid., p. 209.

10. Sutton and Sutton, p. 248.

Chapter 2. Search for a New Trade Route

1. James A. Williamson, "The John Day Letter," *The Cabot Voyages and Bristol Discovery Under Henry VII*, 1962, <www.heritage.nf.ca/exploration/johnday.html> (January 7, 2003).

2. Samuel Eliot Morison, *The European Discovery of America: The Northern Voyages A.D. 500–1600* (New York: Oxford University Press, 1971), p. 289.

3. Clements R. Markham, *The Journal of Christopher Columbus and Documents relating to the Voyages of John Cabot and Gaspar Corte Real* (New York: Burt Franklin, Publisher, 1893), p. 301.

4. Ibid., p. 348.

5. Ibid., p. 378.

6. Andrea Barrett, *Voyage of the Narwhal* (New York: W. W. Norton & Company, 1998), p. 42.

Chapter 3. Brave Explorers in Small Ships

1. Philip Vail, *The Magnificent Adventures of Henry Hudson* (New York: Dodd, Mead & Company, 1965), p. 183.

2. Pierre Berton, *The Arctic Grail* (New York: Viking, 1988), p. 30.

3. Leslie H. Neatby, *In Quest of the Northwest Passage* (New York: Thomas Y. Crowell Company, 1958), p. 35.

4. Ibid., p. 35.

5. Ibid., p. 37.

6. Glyndwr Williams, *The British Search for the Northwest Passage in the Eighteenth Century* (London: Longmans, Green and Co., Ltd., 1962), p. 176.

7. Ibid., p. 196.

8. Ibid., p. 203.

9. Ibid., p. 204.

10. Ibid., p. 210.

Chapter 4. Sir John Barrow's Push for Arctic Exploration

1. Pierre Berton, *The Arctic Grail* (New York: Viking, 1988), p. 27.

2. Ibid., p. 29.

3. Ibid., p. 31.

4. Ibid., p. 39.

5. Ann Savours, *The Search for the North West Passage* (New York: St. Martin's Press, 1999), p. 56.

6. Berton, p. 43.

7. William Edward Parry, *Journal of a Voyage for the Discovery of a North-west Passage from the Atlantic to the Pacific* (New York: Greenwood Press, 1968), pp. 101–102.

Chapter 5. Overland Search for the Northwest Passage

1. Ann Sutton and Myron Sutton, *Journey Into Ice: John Franklin and the Northwest Passage* (New York: Rand McNally & Company, 1965), p. 121.

2. Ann Savours, *The Search for the North West Passage* (New York: St. Martin's Press, 1999), p. 70.

3. John Franklin, *Thirty Years in the Arctic Regions* (Lincoln: University of Nebraska Press, 1988), p. 74.

4. Sutton and Sutton, p. 153.

5. Savours, p. 74.

6. Ibid., p. 78.

Chapter 6. Four Arctic Winters

1. M. J. Ross, *Polar Pioneers, John Ross and James Clark Ross* (Montreal: McGill-Queen's University Press, 1994), p. 142.

2. Ibid., p. 150.

3. Ibid., p. 151.

4. Ibid., p. 157.

5. Ibid., p. 161.

6. Ibid., p. 163.

Chapter 7. Along the Coast of North America

1. Pierre Berton, *The Arctic Grail* (New York: Viking, 1988), p. 132.

2. William Barr, *From Barrow to Boothia: The Arctic Journal of Chief Factor Warren Dease, 1836–1839*, <http://www.ric.edu/rpotter/dease.html> (February 19, 2003).

Chapter 8. Search and Discovery

1. Pierre Berton, *The Arctic Grail* (New York: Viking, 1988), p. 218.

2. Ibid., p. 225.

3. Ibid., p. 232.

4. Brendan Lehane, *The Northwest Passage*, (Alexandria: Time-Life Books, 1981), p. 150.

5. C.B. Sherard Osborn, *The Discovery of the North-West Passage by HMS "Investigator," Apt. R. M'Clure*, (London: Longman, Brown, Green, Longmans, & Roberts, 1857), p. 291.

6. Sir John Franklin, <www.britannica.com/eb/article?idxref=29347> (May 5, 2001).

Chapter 9. Navigating the Passage

1. James P. Delgado, *Across the Top of the World*, (New York: Checkmark Books, 1999), p. 171.

2. Pierre Berton, *The Arctic Grail* (New York: Viking, 1988), p. 538.

3. Ibid., p. 539.

4. Brendan Lehane, *The Northwest Passage*, (Alexandria: Time-Life Books, 1981), p. 163.

5. Roald Amundsen, *The North West Passage: Being the Record of a Voyage of Exploration of the Ship "Gjoe" 1903–1907 by Roald Amundsen With a Supplement by First Lieutenant Hansen Vice-Commander of the Expedition* (New York: Dutton and Company, 1908), p. 125.

6. Berton, p. 545.

Chapter 10. The Northwest Passage on the Map

1. Pierre Berton, *The Arctic Grail* (New York: Viking, 1988), pp. 542–543.

2. On the Land, Northwest Passage Territorial Park, 2002, <http://www.nunavutparks.com/on_the_land/ northwest_passage_park_activities.cfm> (April 18, 2003).

★ Further Reading ★

Beattie, Owen, John Geiger, and Shelley Tanala. *Buried in Ice*. New York: Scholastic/Madison Press Book, 1992.

Blashfield, Jean F. *Jacques Cartier in Search of the Northwest Passage*. Mankato, Minn.: Compass Point Books, 2001.

Curlie, Lynn. *Into the Ice: The Story of Arctic Explorations*. New York: Houghton Mifflin Co., 1998.

Doak, Robin Santoes. *Henry Hudson Searches for the Northwest Passage*. Mankato, Minn.: Compass Point Books, 2003.

Gaines, Ann Graham. *Captain Cook Explores the Pacific*. Berkeley Heights, N.J.: Enslow Publishers, Inc. 2002.

Lawlor, Laurie. *Magnificent Voyage: An American Adventurer on Captain Cook's Final Expedition*. New York: Holiday House, 2002.

Mason, Antony. *Perry and Amundsen: Race to the Poles*. Orlando, Florida: Raintree Steck-Vaughn, 1995.

Meltzer, Milton. *Captain James Cook: Three Times Around the World*. New York: Benchmark Books, 2002.

★ INTERNET ADDRESSES ★

Ocean Explorer: Arctic Explorations. National Oceanic and Atmospheric Administration. 2002. <http://oceanexplorer.noaa.gov/explorations/02arctic/welcome.html>.

"Pathfinders & Passageways: The Exploration of Canada." National Library of Canada. <http://www.nlc-bnc.ca/explorers/index-e.html>.

Potter, Russel A. *Franklin in the Public Eye: 1818–1859.* 2002. <http://www.ric.edu/rpotter/publiceye.html>.

★ INDEX ★